Family Walks
in Leicestershire

Meg Williams

Meg Williams

HIGH INTEREST · LOW MILEAGE

Scarthin Books of Cromford
Derbyshire
1995

For my husband Clive, who shares my love of Leicestershire, especially Burrough Hill Fort where our story began and Seagrave where the badger ignored us!

THE COUNTRY CODE

Guard against all risk of fire
Fasten all gates
Keep dogs under proper control
Keep to paths across farmland
Avoid damaging fences, hedges and walls
Leave no litter
Safeguard water supplies
Protect wildlife, plants and trees
Go carefully on country roads
Respect the life of the countryside

Published by Scarthin Books, Cromford, Derbyshire, 1995

Phototypesetting by Paragon Typesetters, Queensferry, Clwyd

Printed by Redwood Books

Illustrations and photographs all by Meg Williams

Maps by Ivan Sendall

Cover photograph: Bradgate Ruins by Guy Cooper

ISBN 0 907758 82 7

Deer in Bradgate Park (Route 13)

Preface

Leicestershire's countryside offers a variety of enchantment but keeps its real treasures hidden from the casual observer. *Walking the county*, however, reveals unsuspected loveliness everywhere.

The scenery ranges from spacious uplands, broad valleys and gently rolling farmland to craggy granite hillside, varied woodland and sparkling water. Many of its delights are relatively unknown . . . except to the Leicestershire foxes of course, of which you are likely to catch at least a glimpse if you go quietly! You can be sure they will observe you!

The Romans built their Leicester from local clays, so it is not surprising that brick of various shades remains common when it comes to buildings but you will also find lots of half-timbering (sometimes with brick-infill or 'nogging'), orange, red and golden ironstone and some cold grey limestone as well as the multi-coloured Charnwood granite and greeny-blue Swithland slate. The variety of building styles and materials will delight the explorer prepared to look beyond the obvious. As always, attractive vernacular architecture offers echoes of its setting, its source and its purpose.

Mercifully, industry has never overpowered the countryside here . . . and nature has healed some scars, ancient and modern. Always primarily a farming and hunting county, Leicestershire has been fortunate, though today motorways scythe threateningly, reminding us to enjoy its enchantments whilst we may!

Happy exploring!

About the author

Meg Williams, former deputy headteacher, lives on the edge of Charnwood Forest and since taking early retirement some years ago has been busy walking and recording in words and pictures the local history and natural wildlife of Leicestershire. In turn this has led to illustrated articles on the British countryside for the local and national press and pictures for both public and private collections at home and abroad.

Despite the illness which caused her retirement Meg also found time to produce a children's book on badgers for the National Federation of Badger Groups and she continues to produce walks' guides for the Leicester Mercury.

Acknowledgements

My grateful thanks to Doctors John and Jacqui for route-sampling, endless encouragement . . . and not least for keeping me alive and well enough to walk!

Contents

Map of Area

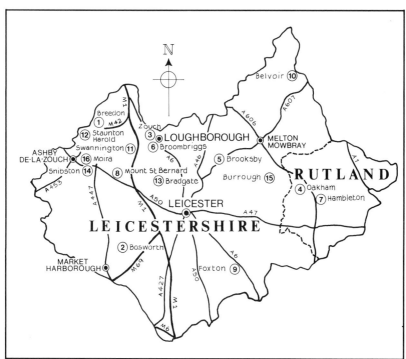

Grand Union Canal (Route 9)

Introduction

The walks in this book are chosen with families in mind, so for the most part they include something with interest for and within the capabilities of, all age groups. Almost without exception opportunities exist for shortening, diverting into civilisation for rest, tea or interest; or even for 'golden oldies' to sit and watch the world go by while more energetic family members explore! Equally there are opportunities to avoid civilisation and for more demanding walking for those inclined, so with a little preliminary consultation all tastes − and ages − can hopefully be accommodated.

Choosing a walk

For those unused to walking and for very young children obviously it is advisable to choose fairly easy walks first, or just to sample the particularly easy parts of longer walks, never, of course, omitting the 'natural break', be it tea or recreation ground, shops or exhibition. It is better to over-estimate the time required in order to allow plenty of time for rest, play, exploration, and re-living some of the history you will inevitably encounter, not to mention savouring the scenery.

Although it is assumed that each walk will take up the largest part of a day's outing it is possible to combine some of the walks, or aspects of two different walks where age, ability and interest allow or demand such extension.

Allowing sufficient time

Where small children and walking are concerned much depends on the parents! Make it interesting and tiredness and demands to 'carry me' will not become a problem, always provided you are realistic in your expectations. A pace of around a mile an hour for the very young is probably the most you can expect . . .slow down, enjoy re-discovering the world with the eyes of a tiny child, it is a magical place! . . . a magnifying glass in your pocket will help ensure fascinating rest periods for all concerned whilst binoculars offer yet another view for older members of the family.

What to Wear

A walk can be made or marred by what you wear. Sturdy, comfortable walking shoes, boots or wellingtons (though the latter can be hot and uncomfortable on long walks) mean you are sure − and dry − footed. Carrying waterproof outer garments is essential in Britain and several inner layers, e.g. shirt and thin jumpers, allow for changes from cold to hot and back again! Caps and woolly hats ensure you don't lose a precious quarter of your body heat in cold weather and sunhats covering the nape of the neck are a must in summer.

A backpack of some sort will carry food and drink, plasters, spare clothes, maps, guides, gloves, etc., and leave hands free. A walking stick can be useful to clear the way should paths become somewhat overgrown but by and large Leicestershire's paths are well walked and cared for. If for any reason you find a footpath obstructed take the shortest possible detour to regain the path and report the obstruction to Leicestershire Waymark 2000 at County Hall on Leicester 657086 or to the

Leicestershire branch of the Rambler's Association, Loughborough 890779 (evenings).

Refreshments
Most Leicestershire pubs allow children accompanied by adults, some have beer gardens and play areas and many are situated by village greens or other such open space. If packed lunches are carried remember that most landlords do not approve of such food being consumed on their premises. Many pubs are open all day now but even so possible closing times should be borne in mind, as with teashops, many of which close by five o'clock. The Route guide indicates where such establishments close for the winter season.

Public Transport
Although it is assumed that most families will travel by car, the starts of some walks can be reached by 'bus. Details of the local services operating in the area (which are prone to frequent change) are given in the appendix together with addresses and telephone numbers of the 'bus operators covering Leicestershire. The best option is to 'phone BUSLINE on 01162 511411 when planning your outing. The 'Guide to Public Transport in Leicestershire' produced by Leicestershire Tourism may also be helpful.

With telephone numbers about to change coinciding with publication I have endeavoured to give you the up-dated numbers but you may find the following useful:

The Nottingham prefix 0602 will become 01159

The Leicester prefix 0533 will become 01162

In general other area codes change by 0 becoming 01.

Entrance to the first Oakham School (Route 4)

Map Key

→ → – – → – –   Route. All routes follow public rights of way and, on occasions, include concessionary footpaths

· · · · · · · · · ·   Route variations

═══════════   Road

⋙⋙⋙   Old railway track

—+—+—+—+—   Railway track

∿∿∿∿   Stream or brook

—)(—   Bridge

🌲🌳🌲🌳🌲🌳   Woodland, pine and deciduous

✠   Church

■   Building

①   Number corresponds with route description

〰〰〰   Canal, river, etc.

∖∣∖∣∖∣∣∣∣∕∕   Earthworks, bulwarks etc.

P   Parking

✗   Picnic benches

Ⓣ   Toilets

Breedon-on-the-Hill

Outline
Breedon War Memorial and Green − Rambler's Cottage − Bulwarks and Church − Quarry − Lock-Up − Rambler's Cottage − Green.

Summary
This walk offers the site of an Iron Age fort, important sculpture from a Saxon Abbey, the remains of an Augustinian Priory, views of the deep, deep galleries of a quarry still working after 2,000 years, a village 'Lock-Up', picturesque cottages and a Garden Centre with a difference.

Initially there is a short steep climb with strategically placed seats but thereafter it is all easy walking. To avoid the sharpness of the rise you can take your car up to the Church car park via the signposted 'Motor Road to Church' and make the Church your starting point. Stout shoes and trousers are advisable, the path is narrow and can be muddy. The Church itself is open daily: summer 9.00 to 6.00, winter 9.00 to 4.00.

Attractions
This walk plucks you from the comfortingly modern world at the foot of Breedon Hill, depositing you high on the strange and windy mount known as 'The Bulwarks'. This unique and atmospheric spot has, since at least the 3rd C. BC., known both good and evil, Christian and Pagan.

Half of the hill has been devoured by quarrying begun in the Iron Age and which relatively recently has swallowed up ancient enclosures and earthworks, monastic cells, even a Saxon cemetery. Lately public pressure has prevented it gobbling up the remaining 'half-a-hill' and the precious Church . . . though only just, as the nearness of the gaping gash to the churchyard wall testifies. No room for complacency either, look down into the vast chasm below and you will see matchstick men and matchbox machinery quarrying still!

Breedon takes its name from two words both meaning hill, the Celtic 'bre' and the Old English 'dun'. In 516 A.D. St. Haroulph, an early Christian hermit, lived on this hilltop. In 676 A.D., a Saxon named Friduric founded a Church close by the site of today's Church.

The strange and solitary hill was given by King Aethelred of Mercia to the monks of Peterborough to found a monastery which was duly dedicated in 676. Incredibly the precious Saxon carvings of humans, beasts, birds, plants and geometric designs (and what is said to be the finest surviving Saxon sculpture in Europe, the Breedon Angel) from that early monastery, grace today's Church.

In 731 a Breedon monk, Tatwin, became Archbishop of Canterbury. He was fond of writing rhymes and riddles . . . try solving this one of his:

> My strength lies in two arms.
> I have great confidence that I can grasp with my gaping jaws
> Unalarmed by anything hard, rough or hot.
> With jaws gaping fearlessly, I try to seize all things''.

the answer? . . . . a pair of tongs!

The monks of Breedon produced illustrated manuscripts and their designs must have been influenced by the stonework carvings we can see today. Those carvings, whether inside or outside the earlier building, were painted by the monks in the same jewel-like colours as their manuscripts and their monastery must have been a magnificent sight from the plain below, glowing with colour atop its lonely hill. By comparison, today's Church is starkly grey and gloomy.

Before leaving its environs, scan the panoramic view. It includes Charnwood Forest's highest point, Bardon Hill. At 912 feet, no higher point is reached in a straight line East until the Ural mountains in Russia . . . the wind sometimes blows very cold up here!

Your footpath round the boundary of the quarry workings gives a glimpse of the extent of this 400′ upthrust of Carboniferous Limestone, rich in fossils. Bluebells, honeysuckle, travellers' joy and rabbits abound in season, but down in the village the 'Lock-Up' offers a change in mood as you imagine incarceration, however temporary. Escape such thoughts by visiting the Priory Nurseries next to the war memorial green. You will be able to feed mallard, browse amongst crafts and books, pick produce, buy garden goodies or best of all savour home-made cakes and tea!

Breedon Lock-up

11

Route 1

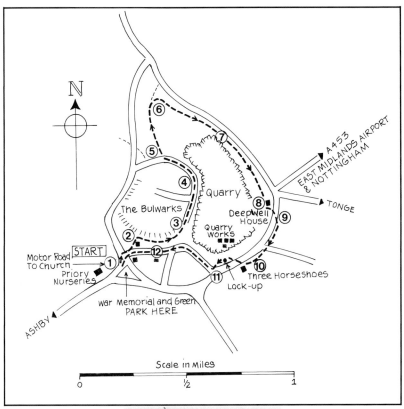

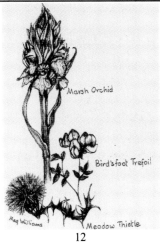

Marsh Orchid

Bird's foot Trefoil

Meadow Thistle

Meg Williams

12

Route 1

Breedon-on-the-Hill   3 miles

Start

War Memorial Green at Breedon-on-the-Hill on the A453 not far from the well-signposted East Midlands Airport. Park sensibly around the green. If using the alternative start at the Church follow the signposted 'Motor Road to the Church' from the War Memorial Green and park in the Church car park. GR 404229. Landranger Map 129 applies.

Route

1. *With the stone-cross-topped War Memorial to your right follow the 'Motor Road to the Church' briefly, then turn right down Hollow Lane past aptly named 'Rambler's Cottage'.*

2. *Turn left immediately after 'Cherry Orchard' passing up the sign-posted footpath. Where the wide track sweeps round towards a cream-coloured house take the narrow beige footpath to the left, it offers a welcome seat partway up.*

3. *Ignore the footpath to the right, continuing uphill where another seat awaits. Continue upwards then at the top pass through the stonewall gap to explore the churchyard and Church.*

4. *On leaving the Church turn left at the churchyard gate through which you entered, heading left down the tarmac after looking over the wall opposite to see matchstick men and machinery at work.*

5. *Turn right along the public footpath signposted to Wilson, and right again with it as it bends to run parallel with a road on your left.*

6. *Ignore the 'Public Footpath to Melbourne' sign to the left, golf course greensward lies distantly left. Your path now sweeps right, Breedon Churchtower soon appears slightly right ahead.*

7. *At and after wide metal gates on your right are glimpses of the incredible quarry depth as your footpath carries you safely above road and quarry.*

8. *Pass down towards quarry buildings on your right and the busy main road below, keeping 'Deep Well House' and its cupressus hedge close to your left. Join the road next to the footpath sign.*

9. *Cross the road and then turn right along its pavement in the direction of signposted Lount and Ashby. Tonge lane offers a seat before you go.*

10. *As you sight the 'Three Horseshoes', the old village 'Lock-Up' and Pound lie on the right so cross the road carefully to investigate and prepare to turn right immediately after the 'Lock-Up'.*

11. *Go up 'The Delph' at the 'Footpath to the Church' sign, pass 'Chestnut Close' and follow the tall brick wall round. Ignore the footpath sign to the right. Continue, keeping to the right where the tarmac lane forks.*

12. *Pass Hillfoot Cottage on your left. Soon you will reach 'Cherry Orchard'. Watch for 'Rambler's Cottage' on your left, then turn left heading towards the 'Holly Bush' Pub and beyond the green and its war memorial.*

Refreshments
The Priory Nurseries weekdays: 10.00-4.30pm, weekends: 11.00-4.30pm, the Holly Bush or Three Horseshoes public houses.

Hollybush Inn

14

Meg Williams

The Church, Breedon-on-the-Hill

Bosworth Battlefield

Outline
Battlefield Centre — Shenton Station — King Richard's Field — Ashby-de-la-Zouch Canal — Ambion Wood — King Richard's Well — Battlefield Centre.

Summary
Easy walking offering the well-signed site of a medieval battle which changed the course of English history; an old railway station and cutting; towpath and tiny aqueduct; woodland and wildlife and the sadly evocative well where a King drank prior to the battle which was to leave him horse-less, coronet-less and lifeless!

The route includes a short stretch of pavementless country road walking on the very quiet road between King Richard's Field and the Aqueduct.

Attractions
This walk transports you back in time to the 22nd August, 1485. On that day this greensward trembled under the thundering hooves of gallant horses, and the air was rent by the rallying cries of determined knights and the death rattles of their fallen comrades.

On Ambion Hill the armies of the ruling Plantagenet King of England, Richard III, and the Lancastrian claimant to the Throne, Henry Tudor, fought one of this country's most important battles, the Battle of Bosworth.

Here Richard, last of the Yorkist Kings, died and here Henry became King of England, ending the thirty years of feuding between Yorkists and Lancastrians known the 'Wars of the Roses'. Here ended the Middle Ages and began the Tudor dynasty. This was also the last battle in which a King personally led his knights against the foe.

Don't miss the superb Battlefield Exhibition — £2.00 adults, £1.30 children. It has lifesize models and tableaux, a large scale mock-up of the battlefield and a film theatre showing the battle scenes and death of Richard III from the famous film.

Parking costs 50p, all amenities are close at hand and the tables and views make it a pleasant picnic spot. If grandparents, the disabled, or the disinclined are with you they can happily stay in or near the car, watch the world go by, visit the well-stocked shop or enjoy delicious home-made cakes and tea in the Buttery Cafeteria whilst you walk. Remember however that it opens for the summer season only, although the Country Park, etc., is open all year during daylight. Tel: 01455 290429 for details.

Partway round, the old Shenton Station offers information and souvenirs, drinks and ice-cream and has another car park and toilets, but check on opening times before leaving the Baattlefield Centre. There are superb picnic spots wherever you go on this walk if you carry your own food and drink. Some weekends a limited train service links the Station with Market Bosworth and Shackerstone Station which has a Museum of Railwayana. Telephone 01827 880754 or 01827 715790 for further information .

After sampling the tranquillity of towpath and — in season — spotting birds;

brimstone, peacock, common blue, wall brown and hairstreak purple butterflies; meadowsweet and early purple orchid in Ambion Wood, now a Nature Reserve, you will find yourself back into the battletorn past at the site of King Richard's left flank and his Well.

On the way home call at the little Church of Sutton Cheney — Richard's pre-battle prayers there may not have helped him but you will be intrigued by the surprising number of written and fresh flower tokens from present-day supporters (from home and abroad) tucked around the commemorative plaque to his memory.

King Richard's Well

17

Route 2

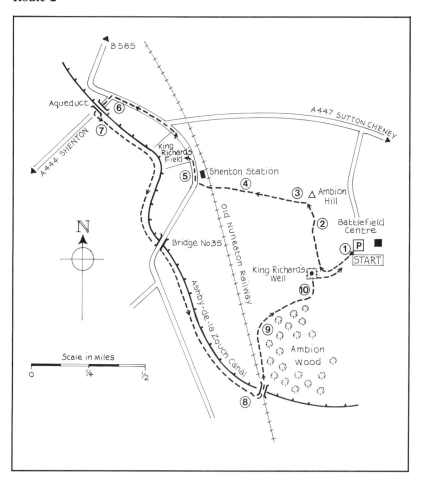

Route 2

Bosworth Battlefield

Start

Bosworth Battlefield Centre close to the A.5, A.444, A.447 and the B.585 and signposted from each in the vicinity of Market Bosworth. The Exhibition Centre and Cafeteria open Monday to Friday inclusive from 1.00 to 5.00 p.m. and Saturdays, Sundays and Bank Holiday Mondays from 11.00 to 6.00 p.m. Park in Exhibition Centre Car Park. OS Landranger Map 140 (Leicester and Coventry area). GR 401003. This is sheep country so please keep your dog on a lead at all times.

Route

1. *From the car park head slightly downhill towards the iron gate into the fenced area around King Richard's Well but do not enter, for that is your exit later. Instead, with your back to the gate, turn left to follow the wooden fencing as it rises to the top of the slight hill.*

2. *At the sign on the fence to your left 'Path 5 to Ambion Hill' , follow the gravel path and pass 'King Richard's Vanguard' and 'Richard's Command Position'. Continue following the path round left and downhill.*

3. *Pass 'The Position of the Stanley Forces' and 'The Charge', then go through the wooden gate on your right, heading downhill and leaving 'Henry Tudor's Front Line' on your left.*

4. *Pass through another wooden gate, and another, then a third seven yards away – a 'Heart of the Battle' sign is on your left and a standard flies proudly. The bed of the old Nuneaton Railway's Shenton Cutting (now restored as the Bosworth Light Railway, so cross with care) and Shenton Station lie ahead plus car park and Portaloos.*

5. *Turn right along the road outside the Station to reach a wooden gate marked 'To King Richard's Field'. Diagonally across the field lies a steep wooden-stepped path to a grassy, secluded possible picnic spot beside the canal. Explore King Richard's field, then rejoin the road, continuing left along it to the Shenton turn.*

6. *Turn left to Shenton, the canal-carrying aqueduct lies ahead of you. Pass under it and turn immediately left to take the Ashby Canal footpath which passes up its bank (close to the Birchmoor Angling Club sign).*

7. *Turn right at the top to pass along the towpath, going under Bridge No. 35 (unless you wish to shorten the walk by passing up to the road and turning right towards the Battlefield standard, going thence back to the Battlefield Centre). Continue the walk by following the towpath. Ambion Wood will lie on your left on the opposite side of the canal.*

8. *At the old metal-sided railway bridge over the canal take the wooden handgate on your right, turn immediately left, passing over the wooden-planked bridge to reach a pathway alongside the Woods.*

9. *Descend the wide grassy track at the woodland edge, following as it narrows and bends round uphill to the right. Pass through the handgate near a sign saying 'Ambion Wood, Battle of Bosworth Field', continuing along the rust coloured path, passing 'The Marsh' and 'Richard's Left Flank' signs.*

10. *Go through the handgate to Richard's Well, then pass up the slight rise ahead to reach the Battlefield Centre.*

Sutton Cheney Church

Timber Framed Cottage, Soar Lane (Route 3)

Zouch Cut

Outline
Canal Bridge − Pasture Lane − Sutton Bonington − Soar Lane − River Soar − Zouch Cut − Zouch Mill − car

Summary
Easy flat walking (apart from the tiny hump of the canal bridge!) on footpath, track, lane, village street, riverside and towpath. A variation halves the walk but eliminates the prettiest part of the riverside. The few yards you walk by the A.6006 is pavemented.

Attractions
Today's gaunt grey mill dominates the tiny hamlet of Zouch but its Domesday mill was the most valuable on the River Soar. Now the one-time mill earns its living from the flats created within and the mill race is sadly silent. The name 'Zouch' probably derives from the Old English 'sot', meaning wooden or foolish, perhaps originating from a comment on an early bridge for throughout the centuries the area has been notorious for flooding.

A hump-backed canal bridge, lost and lonely in the middle of a field, heralds a walk which takes you to the fascinating village of Sutton Bonington where swings and a play area offer amusement for small children . . . and a seat for parents!

Sutton Bonington has twin churches and twin river lanes, for it is really two villages grown into one. The first, Pasture Lane, offers a general stores (until recently a working forge) which sells a useful booklet 'Discovering Sutton Bonington Past and Present' produced by the village's own Local History Society.

Of the two churches St. Anne's is my favourite, small, hidden and uniquely beautiful, probably originating in the 11th C. The later, larger St. Michael's has Victorian stained glass windows by Kempe. Soar Lane, the second river-lane, has a 1661 jettied, timber-framed cottage with later framework-knitting workshop windows to its first floor. Here yarn was given out to homeworkers from surrounding villages and needles and equipment stocked and sold.

Imagine this quiet old lane as the busy thoroughfare it once was, with horse-drawn carts taking coal to the village from narrowboats and barges moored at the point where it meets today's willow-framed river. You pass a boatyard, which has been home to two of Dunkirk's valiant 'little ships' and their owners for many years, 'Monarch' may have moved on but the 'St. George' should still be there.

Zouch Cut, a short cut created by the canal-makers turned the ancient mill hamlet of Zouch into an island. Nearby Zouch Bridge built in 1930 spans the waters, linking Leicestershire and Nottinghamshire. An earlier bridge was still known as 'Sott's Bridge' in 1622 harking back to the medieval name of the settlement. Records show that a stone packhorse bridge existing in the 1200's needed repair in 1358. Doubtless the very first bridge was wooden and responsible for the name 'sot' with its meaning of wooden and foolish!

Finally a canalside pub, the 'Rose and Crown' offers moored boats, picnic tables, opportunist mallard and welcome refreshment!

St Anne's Church. Sutton Bonington

Route 3

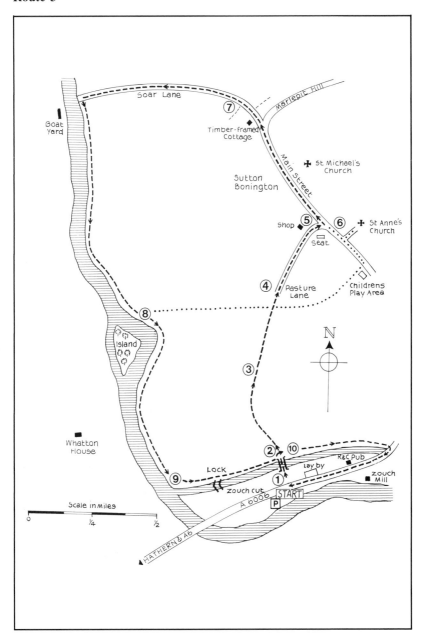

Route 3

Zouch Cut   5¼ miles, variation: 3¼ miles

Start

From the A.6 at Hathern near Loughborough take the A.6006 to Zouch. Almost a mile along you can park off the road on the right at a large 'P' sign or further on in a layby on the left by a telephone kiosk. GR 505233. Landranger Map 129 applies.

Route

1. *Take the 'Bridlepath to Sutton Bonington' opposite the blue 'P'. Ahead you will see the stone canal bridge over which you pass.*

2. *Once over do NOT turn along the towpath in either direction but continue straight ahead following the footpath, keeping the hedge on your left.*

3. *Ignoring the 'Bridlepath to Zouch' allow the power pylons to march with you on your left and follow the path as it widens to a cart track. Glimpse the grey of Whatton House left.*

4. *Follow the track past a blue waymark, it then becomes tarmac and grit. Pass over a brick bridge and presently the track grows to become Pasture Lane with cottages, village store and seat.*

5. *You may wish to buy the local history book from the stores and divert where Pasture Lane meets Main Street to explore more of the village, (particularly St. Anne's Church), reach the childrens' playground, or take the shorter variation. To reach the Church turn briefly right along the main street then left along St. Anne's Lane.*

   Further to the right along Main Street is the childrens' playground, roughly at the point of the former boundary of the two villages which became one.

   To shorten your walk, cross the tarmac by the play area, going through the gate and across the playing field. Keep close to the right boundary continuing until you reach a ditch with a narrow concrete footbridge. Cross it to the riverside footpath along which you turn left, following route instruction 8 onwards.

6. *To continue the main walk from St. Anne's and the playground return along Main Street, passing Pasture Lane left, to reach St. Michael's Church right. Where the road sweeps round up Marlepit Hill continue straight on into Soar Lane, admiring the 1661 timber-framed cottage with its herringbone brick and jettied first floor. Follow the lane, ignoring footpath sign right.*

7. *Ignore another sign left just after the brick bridge, keep to this river-lane. At the river turn left along the bank keeping the low concrete flood wall to your left. When it ends continue along the towpath to a stile.*

8. *Cross the stile keeping to the river's edge, pass under power lines to another stile. Whatton House glares grimly grey atop its hill right. Cross yet another stile with pylons left and the busy A.6 on the opposite side of the river right.*

9. *Pass under power lines and over another stile, and another, keeping to the river's edge until it sweeps right and the canal cut begins to its left. Follow the sign for 'All Craft' (on dry land!) accompanying the canal round, passing over the small white-marked fence across the towpath to your left (lock gates just beyond).*

10. *Follow the towpath past the canal bridge you crossed earlier and continue, eventually passing the back of the 'Rose and Crown' on the opposite bank. Come out at the road, turning right over the bridge, passing Zouch Mill left and the 'Rose and Crown' right to return to your car.*

Refreshments
The Rose and Crown welcomes children, has good food. picnic tables and canal views. Pasture Lane Stores sells lemonade, crisps, etc.

Canal Cut, Zouch

A Trip Around Oakham

Outline
Castle Outer Bailey – Church – Medieval Chapel – Market Place – Castle – County Museum – Dog Kennel Cottage – Viking Way – Outer Bailey

Summary
An easy walk through what was – to many still is – the county town of Rutland, England's smallest, most attractive county!

Exploration of the grassy outer bailey (which once contained the castle fishponds and now offers play area and bandstand) is followed by investigation of Church, school, medieval Chapel, the Castle's hall and its unique collection of royal horseshoes, and a wonderful rural museum before the crossing of field and meadow, with glimpses of Rutland Water and Burley Hall before returning along the Viking Way.

Attractions
The mellow stone and sculpture of the Norman castle hall, its horseshoes and its gemlike setting in emerald greensward hint at Oakham's rare treasures. Hidden away in its centre is another jewel, a tiny medieval stone chapel, once part of a 12th C. hospital. Its present-day setting of wardened and community-centred flats for the elderly echoes the ancient provision of homes for twelve poor and sick men, a warden and a subwarden.

You see the venerable earliest building of Oakham School, along with others in the Market Place, all still in use. Nearby the Church presents richly carved 14th C. capitals, and the fun of finding one showing an irate gentleman chasing the fox which has stolen his goose!

A low thatched cottage believed to be the birthplace of the Oakham Dwarf (who emerged from an enormous pie served to King Charles I at nearby Burley-on-the-Hill, stepping out when it was cut) precedes a glimpse of today's mansion. High Street offers 'Flore's House', one of the most important surviving medieval buildings in Leicestershire and Rutland, part of it now a shop. Dating from the 1300's with a 12th C. doorway, it belonged to William Flore, Controller of Works at Oakham Castle, whose son became a Speaker of the House of Commons.

The market place houses *five*-holed stocks (stocks being repaired currently, should be back in place by publication) . . . were the natives hereabouts differently formed?

Here too is the covered Town Pump, in what was anciently the Shambles (where butchers sold their wares). Visit the friendly Rutland County Museum – its building was an Indoor Riding School built for the Rutland Yeomanry. A trip to Rutland Farm Park can easily be added to your outing, it lies approximately 200 yards further along the road to Uppingham.

Route 4

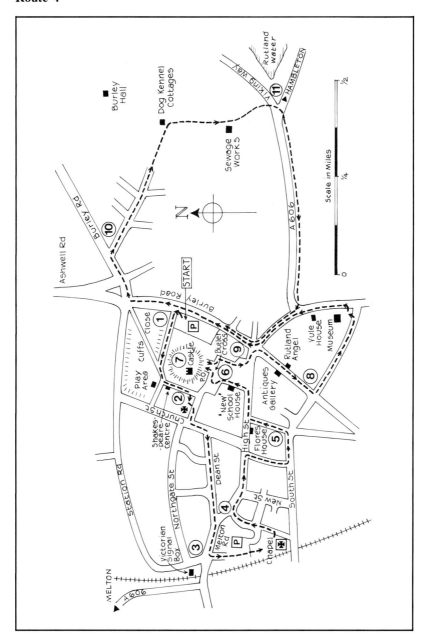

Route 4

A Trip Around Oakham   4½ miles

Start

Follow the A.606 through Oakham Centre to reach the roundabout next to the modern library building. Turn onto Burley Road here, parking on the left outside the Inner Bailey of Oakham Castle. GR 863089. Landranger Map 141 applies.

Route

1. *Head slightly downhill towards the grassy humps and hollows of the Outer Bailey, turning left to join the path towards the bandstands and play area. At the play area turn left along a path which passes the old stone first Oakham School, now its 'Shakespeare Centre'.*

2. *Continue to the Church. Explore, then turn right briefly to reach Church Street, pass left along it to reach the medieval width of Dean Street which brings you to Melton Road. The low thatched cottage where the road narrows is the birthplace of Oakham's famous dwarf.*

3. *Cross Melton Road at the zebra crossing, noting the lovely Victorian signal box at the level crossing, it served as the model for the Hornby model railway sets. Take the little alleyway almost opposite the zebra, passing the Community Centre and reaching a car park. From the car park look for a red brick archway in new housing. It takes you to the medieval stone chapel in the heart of the housing.*

4. *Leave by the archway opposite the chapel door, turning left into Westgate, then right into High street. Building here supplanted the old County Gaol, but a right turn takes you into Gaol Street. Continue to its junction with South Street and the 1700's Quaker Meeting House there. Turn left to reach a passageway on your left (opposite Penn Street) which returns you to High Street.*
   (South Street is worth investigating first, it has some thatched and mud-walled cottages and tile-capped mud walls.)

5. *Go down the passageway (by courtesy of the Congregational Church) to reach the ancient Flore's House on your left. Turn right along High Street until you reach the Market Place on the left with its 'new' schoolhouse of 1857 and other school buildings to the left. Don't miss the old doorway carving showing a ruffed Elizabethan schoolmaster carrying the birch!*

6. *Note the Butter Cross, its unusual stocks and the Town Pump then, keeping the modern Post Office on your left, enter the Castle Bailey (over what would once have been a draw-bridge, shops on your right stand on filled-in moat!).*

7. *Explore the Castle Hall then return to the Market Place, leaving it on the left and crossing the road to enter Mill Street with its 'Rutland Angler' (once the maternity hospital) and 'Antiques Gallery'. Inside the latter you can see (and touch!) its lovely old cruck frame. Notice the 'Titus Oates' opposite, the notorious 1600's plotter and informer was born in Oakham.*

8. *On reaching South Street (again) turn left along it, then left along Catmose Street to reach the Rutland County Museum. Thereafter turn left, passing 'Yule House' (known as the 'Judge's House' — Assize Judges stayed here, processing trumpet-heralded to the Castle via Market Place).*

9. *At the roundabout turn right along Burley Road, pass your car and briefly sample countryside by following Burley Road across the junction, passing more Oakham School buildings on your right. The oldest was the terminus of the Oakham and Melton Canal of 1803, both canal and boats came right into the building.*

10. *Take the second road (into estate housing) to your right, pass straight along to reach a field track leading to 'Dog Kennel Cottage' (Burley's mansion watches on high). Turn right at the cottage through a gate or over its be-nettled stile to pass between two barns and follow the field 'trod' to the cattle-grid and Stamford Road.*

11. *Cross to the opposite verge via the refuge, take the Viking Way footpath to the right, looking back and left for glimpses of distant Rutland Water. The path returns you to the roundabout next to Oakham's Library. Turn right down Burley Road to reach your car.*

Refreshments
Furleys on Burley Road and a host of cafes and pubs en route!

Oakham Castle

30

Brooksby, Hoby and Rotherby

Outline
Rotherby − Brooksby, Church, College and Lost Village − Hoby − Waterhouse and Wreake − Rotherby

Summary
A flat , gentle walk, sometimes muddy, with sturdy but low stiles, three ancient churches, a canalised river and Leicestershire's agricultural and horticultural college which has connections with cardigans and balaclavas! It is wise to take a picnic on this walk, though if you explore Hoby the pub there offers refreshments.

Attractions
Rotherby's churchyard has a sheltered seat and attractive views as well as a Church rivalling the loveliness of its neighbours at Brooksby and Hoby. Brooksby Hall is now the administration hub of the College but has been home to many famous folk, including the Earl of Cardigan who led the 'Charge of the Light Brigade' . . . an event which killed or wounded 247 men and killed over 500 horses.

One of Cardigan's later horses lies buried under a large elm on the lawns. A 19 hands high giant, it died after carrying its master and a pillion-passenger across the nearby Wreake. Our cardigans and balaclavas date back to the Earl, the one being named in tribute to his fancy 'waistcoat' and the other coined to describe the head-swathing adopted by his soldiers to combat the biting cold of the Crimea. The Wreake received its Old Norse name (meaning twisted) from the Danes who settled here in 880 after their defeat by King Alfred (who burnt the cakes!).

Brooksby's Church lies close to the humps and hollows and ridge and furrow of a deserted village. Between 1340 and 1400 Brooksby lost half its population to the Black Plague. Three 'ox-bows' show where the corkscrewing Wreake was straightened for the 1790's Melton Mowbray Navigation which was killed off by the arrival of the railway which survives still. There was a canal lock and basin (wharf) at Brooksby.

Hoby tempts you with an old thatched cottage and you can divert briefly to explore this hamlet and its Church before rejoining the Wreake to pass its Water House (once the office of the M.M.N.) where a chain was fastened across the waterway at dusk to prevent narrowboats moving at night − a dangerous, illegal practice brought about by the pressures of rail competition.

Route 5

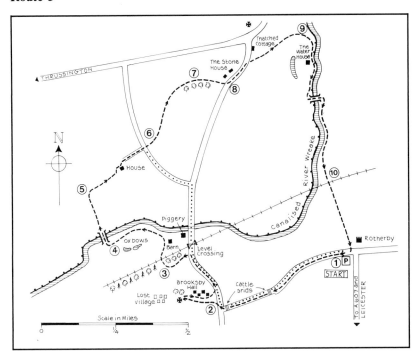

Route 5

Brooksby, Hoby and Rotherby

3½ miles
possible variation 2¾ miles

Start

From the A607 Leicester-Melton road turn left for Rotherby shortly after Rearsby. At the 'T' junction turn towards the village Church, parking sensibly in its vicinity. GR 675165. Landranger Map 129 applies.

Route

1. *With Rotherby Church on your right head downhill to reach the cattle grid marking the 'gated lane to Brooksby'. At the next cattle grid cross the road, entering the grounds of Brooksby College to reach the Church left and the Hall right.*

   Cross the tiny waterfall by the Church, pass alongside the cupressus hedge and go through a handgate into the ridge and furrow fields where you will see the humps and hollows of the lost village.

2. *Retrace your steps to the road outside the College, turning left down it to reach the level-crossing and the College piggery. Turn left just before the crossing re-entering the college grounds through the white handgate with its footpath sign. Walk along the edge of the playing fields to your left, keeping the line of trees and railway line on your right.*

3. *Just after the drinking water stand-pipe on your right you will see a handgate and signs through a gap in the trees. 'Stop, Look and Listen', then if all is clear cross the line and go through the opposite handgate. Be sure to close both handgates. Climb the stile, ignore the footpath sign to your left, turning right and following the field edge round to pass alongside the Dutch barn and bear left, putting the river to your right.*

 From time to time you will see this red, green and blue sign denoting a walk provided by the College for visiting school parties. We follow where it coincides with the public footpath and then desert it, so don't be dismayed when it disappears!

---

4. *Keep to the field edge as it hugs the river round, pass into the next field over the stile, noticing the ox-bows, then turn right, passing over the hump-backed canal bridge via the wooden stile next to the wooden gate.*

5. *Follow the yellow waymark to the field corner ahead, another tall yellow marker guides you. Turn right along the top hedge, ignoring an alternative marker. Pass straight across the field towards a house, Hoby Church sits distantly, slightly left.*

   Yellow-topped posts guide you round the house garden to the drive along which you turn left to reach road.

   To shorten your walk turn right along this road, eventually going over the level-crossing and turning left along the cattle-gridded lane to Rotherby Church.

6. *The main walk takes you across the road to climb the yellow-arrow-and-circle-marked stile opposite. Head straight across the next field, Hoby spire is ahead of you. Climb another stile, plastic greenhouses lie right. Follow the arrow — slightly left towards the Church spire and next field.*

7. *Head towards the first large tree in the hedge for the next stile. Pass over and slightly right towards the Church then follow the line of large trees and stumps down to the bottom left hand corner. Pass over the little brook with its sideless brick bridge, following a farm track briefly as it passes left. Almost immediately, hidden in overhanging hedge right (corrugated barns left), is a yellow waymarked stile into the next field, followed by another taking you onto road.*

8. *Turn left along it towards the Church spire, passing 'Stone House', walking along the high grassy bank on the right. You can divert to explore Hoby by passing the thatched cottage and entering the village. To continue the walk however, follow the footpath sign on the right just before the thatched cottage, and pass into the field at the white-footprinted posts. Head for the river below, then turn right along its bank.*

9. *With the river left you soon reach 'Water House' to pass along the old granite setts between it and the river. Go through the next handgate and continue along the riverbank to reach and pass over the old hump-backed canal bridge. Turn right immediately, keeping to the river on your right now until you reach the railway line near an old red and green corrugated-iron hut.*

10. *'Stop, Look and Listen', then cross the line, passing through the white handgate and over the field to a stile at a rickety handgate. Head uphill to Rotherby's spireless Church (sparing a backward glance at Hoby Church and the old bridge) and the line of the dip in the field will lead you up to the wall of Rotherby churchyard. Walk alongside it to come out at the wooden handgate into the road.*

Brooksby Church

Route 6   **7½ miles**

variation 1: Broombriggs Farm Trail only: 3¼ miles
variation 2: Village and Windmill Hill only: 2¼ miles
variation 3: The Beacon only: 1½ miles

Broombriggs and Woodhouse Eaves

Outline
Beacon Road — Woodhouse Windmill — Broombriggs Hill — Beacon Road — Woodhouse Eaves — Beacon Road — The Beacon — Woodhouse village — Beacon Road

Summary
An uphill and downhill walk . . . or three separate walks, none of them difficult if taken in easy stages making full use of strategically placed seats! It offers part of a farm trail, the remains of a post-mill, a village with pub and craft shop, attractive Charnwood stone and Swithland slate cottages and, finally, brackened countryside leading to trig point and toposcope on the geologically important Bronze Age (or earlier) Beacon Hill.

Sturdy socks, shoes and trousers are recommended in case children inadvertently wander from the pathways into bracken on Beacon Hill. Barelegged locals wander freely but since adders live here it makes sense to keep to the many bracken-free areas and tracks.

Attractions
Windmill Hill has the Charnwood granite skirt of a post mill (in which the entire structure above the skirt pivoted round a massive central post allowing the sails to catch any prevailing wind). It was damaged by severe gales in 1895 and fire in 1945. The windmill's view of Woodhouse Eaves confirms the meaning of the name — it lies on the edge (or 'eaves') of woodland.

The farm trail with its explanatory sign-boards lends additional interest as you make your way to this picnic-tabled 'top' of the county. You can finish your walk thereafter or continue onto the second variation, passing (or sampling!) Ye Olde Bull's Head on your way to explore the village with its well-stocked gift and craft shop and cottages of multi-coloured Charnwood granite topped with the local blue-grey Swithland slate.

The third part or variation begins by passing up scheduled Beacon Hill, home of pre-historic Leicestershire man, to see the remains of its surrounding bank and external ditch defensive earthworks. Bronze Age finds suggest a habitation date of 2000 − 1400 BC . . . today it is home to trig point and toposcope.

Rock layers here were formed at what was the bottom of the sea 700 million years ago and are composed of crystalline grains of volcanic ash. Each layer is formed of ash which fell to the bottom of the sea and settled during separate volcanic eruptions creating the different colours and sizes of the layers which characterise Charnwood granite, differences which indicate the likely involvement of several different volcanoes. These crags have helped geologists decide what the world was like 700 million years ago.

The oddly shaped Frying Pan Pond, along with other wet areas on the Beacon, provides spawning ground for smooth newt and − more rarely − palmate newt. On warm days the rocks above the pond sport sleepy sunbathing adders − and their future meals, common lizards.

Adders only bite in self-defence and flee if disturbed. Like all the flora and fauna on the Beacon they are protected and should not be disturbed. Your routes both up and down the Beacon are wide, well-used tracks well clear of their habitat, thus safeguarding their well-being and your own.

Mill Lane, Broombriggs

Route 6

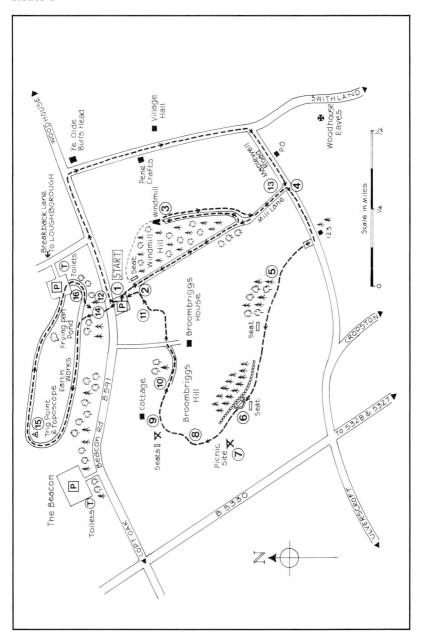

Route 6

Broombriggs and Woodhouse Eaves

7½ miles
variation 1: 3¼ miles
variation 2: 2¼ miles
variation 3: 1½ miles

Start

From Leicester take the B.5327 to Anstey where you turn right onto the B.5328 to Cropston, then left onto the B.5330. Finally turn right towards Woodhouse Eaves on the B.591 (Beacon Road). Ignore Beacon Car Park signs and drop down the hill. Towards the bottom on the right is the sign for Broombriggs Car Park where a contribution to the collection box is requested. GR 524144. Landranger Map 129 applies.

Route

1. *Go through the handgate at the side of the car park, following the worn trod ahead and upwards. Pass through the next handgate at the five-bar gate, heading across the field and uphill to reach the yellow-marked gate at the woodland edge.*

2. *Pass into the woodland at the handgate, ignoring the right-hand arrow but noting the nearby seat. A track passes close to it, whilst behind it at the edge of the wood is a narrow, rugged, steep path . . . either route will take you up to the windmill – the wider, easier, track less directly by eventually turning left uphill when it meets another track.*

3. *Leave the windmill by the downhill track, turning left at its 'T' junction to reach the wooden five-bar gate to your left and pass downhill where the track becomes Mill Lane.*

4. *At the village street turn right briefly to reach a bungalow, number 123, with sentinel pines. Go through the wooden handgate opposite, entering a grassy area and heading towards a Broombriggs Trail noticeboard, following yellow markers. Go through the handgate to the left of it and follow the track upwards, bearing round with it to the yellow-marked telegraph pole.*

5. *Turn left uphill keeping the hedge right, ignoring the track straight ahead towards woodland. A seat halfway uphill in memory of Mary Oram offers views before you pass along the edge of a pine wood to a stonewalled corner and another seat.*

6. *At the hilltop take the stile into a triangular walled area with seat, Swithland Reservoir lies distantly below. Pass over a second stile into a field, continuing with woodland and stone wall on your right to a yet higher point.*

7. *Here is a picnic spot, views on three sides and sweet-scented pines to your back. Bradgate's 'Old John' (the tankard shaped stone tower memorial to the miller who liked his drink and was killed by a falling log at a bonfire celebration at the spot) and War Memorial front the panorama.*

8. *To the right of the picnic table a yellow-waymarked stile takes you along the waymarked wall on your right. Where the wall bends right, cross to the left along the top of the ridge to the yellow-marked handgate by a clump of trees opposite. BE ALERT it is easy to miss your route here.*

9. *Pass through the next handgate, crossing to the far fence − there is no footpath down to your right. As you walk the wide ridge at the top of the field bear round to your right hugging the waymarked fence. Another picnic table offers seating and views before you head downhill following the waymarked post and wire fence to reach a handgate tucked into a corner.*

10. *Pass through and down the grassy track with white buildings distantly right, then bear round left to the waymarked handgate at the bottom right. Pass through to another Broombriggs Trail noticeboard. Cross the stone-walled track to the handgate opposite and follow waymarks on the 'treepens' across the field*

11. *At the stone wall turn right (horses only left) and at the end of the trees go over the waymarked stile. Bear down following waymark signs to the car park below. The first variation finishes here.*

12. *To continue, turn right at the road and head down past houses to the Bull's Head pub where you turn right to explore the village. You pass Pene Crafts on the right and the village hall on the left. At the bottom of the hill the church on its rock lies uphill again, but you need to turn right by corner shops to go along Maplewell road and reach Mill Lane on the right. Pause at the corner first to admire the slateworkers cottages opposite the Le Fevre Village Stores.*

13. *Pass up Mill Lane taking the track straight ahead to the corner of the wood, going through the wood and handgates to return downhill to the car park. The second variation finishes here.*

14. *To complete the main walk leave the car park to cross the road and enter the Beacon at the footpath opposite. This takes you forward to meet a wide track along which you turn left to follow it uphill to the summit of the Beacon, its trig point and toposcope.*

15. *Explore, then return to the wide track and follow it as it swings round and down, passing Frying Pan Pond on your right. Look back from this point to gain an impression of the ancient earthworks (which incorporated some of the rock formations) behind you and slightly left. Continue downhill (ignoring the track to the right) continuing to a second car park and toilets.*

16. *At this car park turn right to pass up between a rhododendron lined track following as it heads across a grassy area. Eventually take the footpath to the left through trees to cross the road and reach Broombriggs Car Park.*
    This completes variation 3 and the main walk.

A Post Mill

Windmill as it would have been

41

Oak in Bradgate Park (Route 13)

Hambleton and Rutland Water

Outline

Hambleton − Rutland Water − Hambleton

Summary

A very easy, pleasant stroll around the edge of an 'almost-island' on the largest man-made lake in Western Europe, now internationally important ecologically, particularly for wintering wildfowl. It is wise to take a picnic on this walk, otherwise the pub in Hambleton is your only option.

Attractions

This walk takes you from lovely old mellow stone houses and green pastures to windy water full of wildfowl and presided over by the 18th C. Normanton Church. t was saved from submergence by Anglian Water and a local Trust which raised its floor level and proofed its masonry prior to the creation of the Reservoir. A causeway was provided giving access to the Church, now a museum of the reservoir's history.

Rutland Water covers 3,100 acres, storing 124,000 million litres of water which is pumped in from the Rivers Nene and Welland. Its maximum depth is 34 metres and it is host to sailors, windsurfers and a passenger cruiser operating out of Whitwell.

High on its hill Burley Hall keeps watch and Hambleton Old Hall, Hambleton Hall and numerous cottages offer architectural interest. Perhaps less welcome are noisy R.A.F. lowflying jets if they happen to be practising.

Across the water lies Barnsdale of B.B.C. gardening renown but the area's greatest attraction has to be its waterfowl. Over 200 different species of birds have been recorded at Rutland Water including ospreys and great northern divers − the winter wildfowl count is around 20,000 birds . . . so take your binoculars . . . and for the sake of the wildfowl and the sheep, keep your dog on a lead at all times. The soothing stillness of the air and the fragrance of the woodland are part of the magic of this walk − so absorb and enjoy!

Rutland Water

Route 7

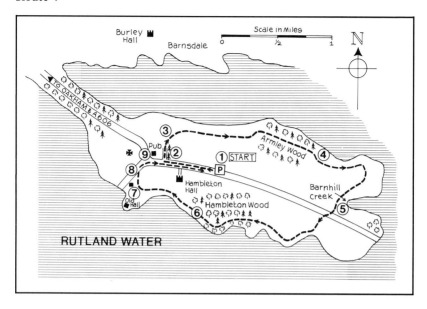

Water Vole

Route 7

Hambleton and Rutland Water   5½ miles

Start

> *From Oakham follow the A.606 Stamford Road and the signs to Rutland Water, taking the 'No Through Road' right fork for Hambleton about a mile from Oakham. Pass through the village with its pub on your left and the Church on the right to park on the wide grass verge by a yellow hydrant just beyond the last of the cottages. GR 904076. Landranger Map 140 applies.*

Route

1. *Once parked, walk back towards the village passing on your left the entrance to Hambleton ('new') Hall, its stableyard and clocktower. Ignore the footpath sign on the right and pass a stone cottage, its ever-alert dog may hurl defiance at you from upstairs leaded-lights!*

2. *With the Church ahead, turn down the footpath signposted on the right opposite a red GR letterbox inset in a cream stone pillar. Go through the wide wooden gate and down the broad grassy track, curtseying low to pass under overhanging pines. House gardens flank you either side.*

3. *Drop down to the beautiful panoramic view of Rutland Water ahead, going through another farm gate and heading to the bottom right hand corner of the field where you pass through a rickety farmgate onto a wide gravel and stone track. Follow this track around to the right as it takes you closer to the water. Burley Hall scowls from slightly left across the reservoir, Barnsdale lies slightly closer. Go over the metal grid, continuing along the track through broadleaved woodland, squirrels will skitter and scatter as you go!*

4. *On over another cattle grid and bear right to follow the track uphill then along to the left. Normanton Church watches distantly from its narrow peninsula refuge whilst on your right the angled thorny shapes of survivor-hawthorns cling to the hillside.*

5. *Follow the track around as it passes over the tail-end of a road (your car waits on a much earlier part of it), passing over the animal grid and into woodland.*

6. *Eventually, after passing recent tree-planting in the woodland edge to your right, you cross another cattle-grid with Old Hambleton Hall sitting ahead and slightly left, snug on its own little peninsula. A white house also appears ahead as you continue.*

7. *As you approach the white house on your right be ready to take the stile into the field on the right just before it. Head up across the field to a stile in the clump of trees roughly opposite the first stile. Pass over and then immediately over another to continue straight ahead, keeping the hedge to your right. The Church spire shows ahead and there are cottages left and right.*

8. *At the wide gate ahead pause to look back at Hambleton Old Hall and Rutland Water before passing through the handgate alongside it, going up the grassy track and reaching the road ahead where you turn right.*

9. *Soon St. Andrew's Church comes up on your left and you turn right at the road junction. In doing so note the picturesque old 'Hambleton Post and Telegraph Office' with its ornate date which I deciphered as 1898 . . . do you? Continue along the road to pass the letterbox on your right and reach your car . . . though I recommend exploring this peaceful, isolated village before leaving.*

Cottage at Hambleton

46

Mount St. Bernard Abbey and Blackbrook

Outline

Mount St. Bernard Abbey − Blackbrook Reservoir − Fenny Springs − Poachers' Corner − Mount St. Bernard Abbey

Summary

A walk including woodlands, a windmill and waterside and some country road. Briefly steep and uneven, it is mostly easy walking, beginning and ending at a monk-made Abbey on what was once bleak and inhospitable land. The monks have a gift shop selling, amongst other things, the pottery they make. Refreshments are not available at the Abbey but the Belfry Pub is nearby and welcomes children. There are toilets at the Abbey.

Attractions

Mount St. Bernard Abbey , established in the early 1800's was the first Cistercian Abbey to be established in England after the Reformation three hundred years earlier. Today the myriad colours of its Charnwood granite walls glimmer and dance in the sunlight in sharp contrast to the stark white simplicity of the interior and the unmarked tomb of the man whose idea it was, Ambrose Phillips de Lisle, a man known for his humility.

The Monastery has welcomed in its time William Wordsworth, Florence Nightingale, Charles Dickens, even royalty; fed thousands of the local poor and lodged many homeless in the 'Potato Famine' of the 1840's. Renowned locally throughout the years for its excellent farm stock and produce the monks also once bred, appropriately enough, St. Bernard dogs.

Walking along the Blackbrook and its Reservoir offers the chance to watch waterfowl and later the restored and converted Fenny Spring Windmill will, hopefully, please your eye. Derelict in the 1950's it now stands proudly atop its hill, testament to the skill of local craftsmen.

You pass close by the site of an ancient Swanimote (open air court for settling manorial and forest-law squabbles) as you return Abbeywards to explore and partake of its peace and tranquillity before heading homewards.

Route 8

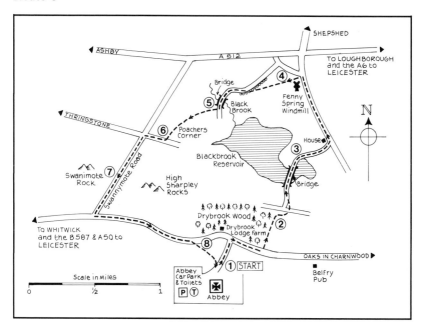

Heron

48

Route 8

Mount St. Bernard Abbey and Blackbrook   5½ miles

Start

Head towards Whitwick on the B587 or through Shepshed on the A512 and follow the Abbey signs. It lies on the Whitwick – Oaks-in-Charnwood road almost opposite Drybrook Lodge Farm. Pass up the Abbey drive and park in the car park. GR 457163. Landranger Map 129 applies.

Route

1. *From the car park walk down the drive, across the Oaks road and turn to the right along its verge. Well before you reach the Belfry Pub take the signed footpath to the left. It will take you down through the edge of woodland following either the yellow, or the yellow-and-red arrows.*

2. *Pass into a field, still following the waymarking and the worn path, the reservoir appears distantly. Continue down to the thick shrubby border of the reservoir and pass over a stile in the nearby stone wall onto a track. Follow the footpath signs, joining a wider track which takes you across a bridge at the narrowest point of the reservoir.*

3. *Continue with the track as it wends away from the water towards a solitary house ahead. Pass by the side of the house to reach a road along which you turn left. Soon you see the sparkling white Fenny Spring Windmill on your left, pass it towards some buildings and a square brick Water Authority building. Close by the building is a yellow-arrowed footpath guiding you into a field.*

4. *Cross it diagonally, following a faint tractor-trail to reach a narrow stonewall aperture onto a tarmac drive. Turn left along the drive and it will bear you round to the left, depositing you on a white-edged bridge.*

5. *Pass over the bridge's pretty brook and almost immediately divert off the drive up a grassy lane to your right. Clear waymarking now guides you up to bear left at the field at the top of the incline. Next follow the boundary and its accompanying worn path round as it moves through a gap into the next field to continue in the same direction as hitherto.*

6. *Turn left at the field corner, following the arrows round the boundary and they will bring you to a metal gate and road where you turn right at this, 'Poacher's Corner' to reach crossroads ahead where you turn left to go uphill.*

7. *Climb this hill with its spinneys and its huge stones on which you can sit a spell. This is Swannymote Road and adjacent are the private rocks, site of the ancient*

49

Swanimote Court. At the 'T' junction with Oaks Road turn left to head towards the Abbey along tarmac footpath on the right side of the road.

8. *Just before Drybrook Lodge Farm there is a footpath through trees on your right, it will take you up through woodland edge to pasture with stunning views and the Abbey drive where you turn right to reach the car park.*

Mount Saint Bernard Abbey

Full walk: 5½ miles
variation 1: Lockside only: 1½ miles
variation 2: Lockside plus Foxton: 3 miles
variation 3: Lockside plus Gumley: 3½ miles

Foxton Locks, Foxton and Gumley

Outline
Foxton Locks and Museum — Foxton Village and Swingbridge — Gumley Village — Foxton Basin — Foxton Locks

Summary
Easy, interesting ramble which can be walked as a whole or as one or more of three variations. The first takes you down by the locks and their feeder pools to the Museum with its working models. The second continues to reach and cross a swingbridge, explore Foxton village (and perhaps its Black Horse pub and a childrens' recreation ground), and return along the towpath to Foxton Basin, (or wharf) its pub and its shops. The third, hardest, circuit takes the towpath to a footbridge and crosses muddy fields to the village of Gumley, returning by bridleway and field to pass up by Foxton's flight of ten locks en route to the car park.

Attractions
Foxton's flight of locks, inclined plane and superb little museum housed in what was the inclined plane's boilerhouse vie for your attention with countryside walking and delightful hamlets. The locks form part of the Grand Union Canal and were built between 1808 and 1814 under the supervision of Thomas Telford. The Market Harborough arm joins the canal at the Basin.

The upward passage through the locks took over an hour so in 1900 the alternative inclined plane method of lifting a boat in a 'bath' was produced. It reduced the time to a mere eight minutes but came too late to survive the railway competition.

Foxton's Church sits where monks anciently worshipped around a Saxon preaching cross dating from at least 850 AD, the remains of which lie inside the Church. The Black Horse Pub almost opposite offers highly rated home-made food and was re-built in its present form in 1900 to accommodate boaters making their way to the new barge-lift.

You may see a narrowboater operating the Swingbridge to allow his vessel through a picturesque lane with lovely old housing. At weekends or Bank Holidays Foxton also offers horse-drawn narrowboat trips from the village to Foxton Locks or vice-versa, you pass the Start points on your walk.

The hamlet of Gumley was the site of an ancient counsel held by the Mercian King Aethelbald in 749 AD so must once have been busy and important. Today's busy central point Foxton Basin offers much of interest for stationary sightseers and refreshment for the hungry!

Route 9

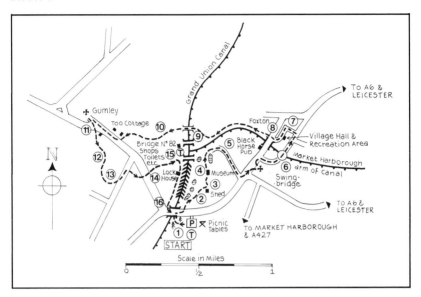

Map labels:

Grand Union Canal

To A6 & LEICESTER

Gumley

Too Cottage — ⑩

⑪

Foxton — ⑧ ⑦

N

Bridge N° 82 — ⑨

Shops Toilets etc. — ⑮ Ⓣ

⑤ Black Horse Pub

Village Hall & Recreation Area

⑫

④ Museum

Market Harborough arm of Canal

Lock House — ⑭

⑬

③

⑥

Swing-bridge

② Shed

⑯

To A6 & LEICESTER

① Ⓣ

P ✗ Picnic Tables

START

To MARKET HARBOROUGH & A427

Scale in Miles

0   ½   1

Foxton Locks

52

Route 9

Foxton Locks, Foxton and Gumley

5½ miles

variations: Lockside only: 1½ miles
Lockside plus Foxton: 3 miles
Lockside plus Gumley: 3½ miles

Start

Take the 'Foxton Locks, Foxton and Gumley' road from the A.427 or the 'Foxton Locks' sign from the A.6 (approx. 4 miles from Market Harborough). Follow the signs until you reach the Foxton Locks car park where there are toilets and a contribution box. GR 692892. Landranger Map 141 applies.

Route

1. *In the car park with the toilets ahead of you, look left for a footpath sign to canal footbridge and Foxton Locks. Pass along this tree-lined path to the footbridge, (which eliminates having to cross the road). Turn right at the canal to go under two bridges and then continue straight ahead, ignoring the footpath round to your right . . . thus placing the canal on your left.*

2. *Balancing feeder ponds for the locks lie left. Your return will be along the towpath opposite but now, noting the richness of the flora, pass left and up and over a small gritty incline. At its 'T' junction (with the Lock House ahead on the opposite side of the canal) turn right on a footpath through an archway of trees.*

3. *Pass the green shed on the right, notice its metalwork plan of the canal ponds. Pass dry canal, bear right to the top of the Incline Plane and its explanatory sign, noting the iron narrowboat hull. With the Incline Plane behind you go down the narrow gravel path signposted 'Canal Museum'.*

4. *Pass down to the canal basin after investigating the Museum. Ignore turning right, going left past the 'Thomas Holt' boat to reach shop and restaurant below. With the canal on your left head along the lane, noting tiny narrowboat gardens.*
   For the very short walk return up the opposite side of the flight of locks following the instructions from 15 onwards.

5. *Notice the footpath signed yellow post as the track swings right taking you uphill away from the canal. At the road turn left to reach the Church. The Black Horse pub lies a few yards past the Church but on leaving the churchyard you need to turn right down Swingbridge Street (really a picturesque lane with cottages and cobbles).*

6. *Pass over the swingbridge, eventually coming to double green wooden gates on the left (saying 'Please Shut the Gate') with stabling behind. Turn left here hugging the brick ivy-clad wall left. Pass along to the wide metal gate ahead and the 'T' junction where you turn left.*

7. *At the next 'T' junction turn left up towards the Church, passing the Village Hall. The white lollipop cycle sign next to it leads immediately to a grassy children's recreation area but you continue along the road as it bends right, ignoring Woodgate straight ahead.*

8. *Pass up to the road junction, a canal bridge lies immediately left (the Black Horse also). Cross this, Middle Street, to pass down to the hedgeline on the left opposite with its footpath sign 'Leicestershire Round—Foxton Locks'. At the canal turn right along the towpath towards Foxton. (Horse-drawn narrowboat trips operate from this point.)*

    Towpath now takes you to Foxton Locks returning you on the opposite bank to the be-gardened narrowboats. Next pass under, then over, the typical Leicestershire 'roving bridge' (which allowed the towing horse to change sides) to reach the pub 'Bridge No. 82' which has toilets for the use of visitors to the area . . . or continue to Gumley without pausing.

    At this point you can shorten the walk by returning up the right hand side of the lock flight, following the instructions from 15.

9. *To continue, retrace your steps over the roving bridge to reach the far bank and turn along it towards Gumley. Take the next footbridge over the canal on your left (ignoring footpath sign right) and head for the yellow-topped post ahead. Continue to the footpath post opposite (about 30 yards to the left of the right hand corner of the field) church spire lies distantly right. Head across for the next yellow-marked post.*

10. *Cross the next stile going left uphill to a metal kissing gate, passing a 'Leicestershire Round' sign and continuing uphill close to post and wire boundary left. Pass alongside cream house to reach the village street where you turn right past 'Too Cottage' to investigate village and Church, noting surviving stable block tower of the Hall demolished in 1964.*

11. *Return down Main Street leaving it via a narrow cobbled Bridleway on the right, going through bridlegate and turning slightly left to reach a hedge-corner by telegraph lines on the left. Keep the lines to your left downhill to hedge below. About 30 yards to their left is the footbridge by a tall mountain ash, its sign may be masked by leaves.*

54

12. *Pass over the double stile to the yellow waymark. After crossing the brook turn left along the worn trod to the corner of the field where you turn right along the post and wire fence keeping it left.*

13. *At the wide gate go into the lane which leads to a road where you turn left, then almost immediately right at the tall bridleway sign. Pass through the gate, crossing the field to the next gate and follow the worn trod, crossing the road when you reach it. Foxton's Lock-keeper's house lies high on the hill ahead right.*

14. *Pass through the next handgate into the field continuing along footpath and keeping to left boundary. Note the ridge and furrow, Foxton's Canal Museum lies further ahead right. Come up to the metal handgate, passing up the track under power lines then follow the power lines on your left.*

15. *Come out onto canal bridge, Foxton's Flight lies right. Turn right at the bottom lock to pass up right hand side of the locks, museum lies left at the other side of the flight of locks and the lock-keeper's cottage close right.*

16. *Turn left over Bridge No. 60, coming down left again to go under the bridge. Next turn left through the wooden gateposts following path (ignoring footpath sign to the right) to retrace your steps along the tree-lined avenue to the car park.*

Foxton Locks

Belvoir Castle

Woolsthorpe Church

Belvoir Castle and Woolsthorpe-by-Belvoir

Outline

Summary

An easy walk incorporating field, village and parkland with grassy track, canal towpath and the possibility of exploring a castle and its sculpture garden and sampling its excellent refreshments in season. Tel: 01476 870262 for details of opening and prices, season is usually March to October. The Chequers at Woolsthorpe and the Rutland Arms (The Dirty Duck) are alternative refreshment stops and the village Post Office offers ice-cream, etc.

Attractions

A beautiful walk overseen by a high-perched fairytale castle as you drop down into its friendly hamlet and sample carefree walking along an abandoned railway line. The former Grantham Railway and Canal Company's branch line (built to transport iron ore from 'Brewer's Grave') takes you gently uphill and downhill to the canal and its 'Dirty Duck' offering panoramic, seemingly uninhabited, scenery.

You will notice ongoing voluntary restoration work on some of Woolthorpe's flight of seven canal locks and catch a glimpse of an ancient drovers' green way . . . the Sewstern Lane. It forms part of today's Viking Way which runs from Stamford to Melton Mowbray. On this walk you sample another section of the Viking Way which connects with the Jubilee Way (which runs from Belvoir to Melton). It is not often you have a taste of three long-distance walks (one at least pre-Roman) in one outing − even if you can't truthfully claim to have walked the length of any!

You will see what is known as 'Brewer's Grave', a brewer from Belvoir Castle was buried here along with his donkey after, reputedly, drowning in a vat of his own beer. Iron ore from here was carried by rail along the old line you walk, part of the Nottingham and Grantham Railway and Canal Company's line leased to the Great Northern Railway. The ore workings, begun in 1879, closed in 1918 and the rail tracks lifted thereafter.

The Vale of Belvoir is beautiful, its people endlessly friendly and its castle wonderful . . . you'll not forget or regret this outing!

Route 10

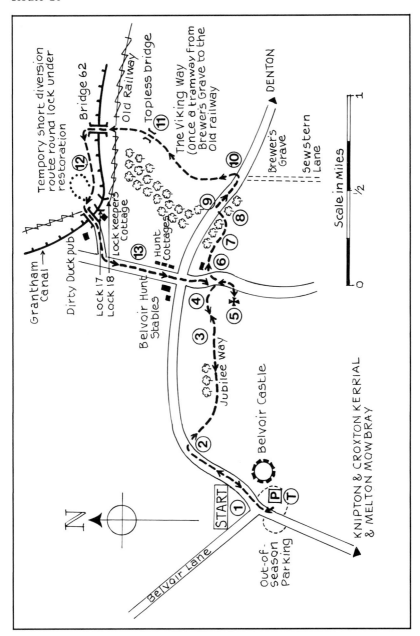

58

Route 10

Belvoir Castle and Woolsthorpe-by-Belvoir   6½ miles

Start

Belvoir Castle lies approximately 12 miles from Melton Mowbray and is well signposted (brown castle) from the A.1, A.52, A.607 and A.46. In season park in the Castle car park, toilets available. There is also a year-round free car park on the opposite side of the road. The season runs from 1st April – 30th September, Castle opens Tues., Wed., Thurs., Sat. 11.00am – 5.00pm (Sundays only in October). Entry to Castle and grounds is £4.25 for adults, £2.65 for children from 5 – 15 inclusive and £3 for senior citizens, but the walk can be undertaken without entering the grounds. GR 818338. Landranger Map 130 applies.

Route

Explore the Castle either before or after the walk . . . in the sculpture garden watch out for the touching small gravestone to 'Happy Manners'.

1. *Park, then with the castle ticket office and entrance behind you turn right along the road towards Belvoir and Woolsthorpe, ignoring the footpath sign opposite the castle entrance.*

2. *After passing a private castle entrance right and rounding the bend turn right along the crown-encircled-orb signed Jubilee Footpath, (Woolsthorpe 1 mile) passing over the stile to the right of the gate. Follow the signs, passing down with castle on the right towards distant Woolsthorpe Church and village. A spasmodic line of oaks lies left.*

3. *Pass over stile following signs, continuing with boundary left, church slightly right. Notice the remains of stone-edged pavement left accompanying the oak survivor line . . . obviously this was once an important path.*

4. *Pass over the next Jubilee Way stile and over the brick bridge and its brook. Bear left round the green track, ignoring footpath sign right. Churchtower lies right and track becomes tarmac, acquiring cottages.*

5. *Notice ornate brick wall on cottage left then turn right towards Chapel Hill to investigate Church before returning downhill to reach the tall freestanding pub sign at a small inlet on the right. Pass up between the houses of the inlet's little cul-de-sac to reach the pub, then leave it behind on your left, keeping to the right hand boundary and heading for the cricket field ahead.*

6. *Pass the pub stables on your right as you go, noting the 'Jubilee Way' symbol on the low square brick building right (faded white lettering proclaims 'Gents'). Head up the right boundary towards cricket score board, behind it lurks your next stile heading you uphill to the corner of the wood opposite.*

7. *Continue to next woodland corner, passing up left hand side of grassy field. Look back for view of castle and Woolsthorpe snug in its valley below. Keep to left boundary, hugging the woodland edge and watching out for a track on the left as you go.*

8. *At the 'Private Tip' sign pass over or through the gate (Jubilee signed on the reverse) to go briefly along a track through the wood, emerging onto road by stepping over the low wooden bar at the side of the gate.*

9. *Turn right along the road for a few yards, just before the bend is a blue road sign at which you turn left to join the Viking Way. First, however, continue to the road bend for a glimpse of the grassy track of ancient Sewstern Lane which continues ahead where the road bends at the point known as Brewer's Grave.*

10. *Return to join the Viking Way, now on your right, and pass along the yellow-helmet-signed track as it becomes grassy and field-edged. At a Viking-signed, blue-arrowed yellow post follow the track as it swings right after a slight climb. Another footpath joins from a left field corner as you continue along this easy − former railway − route. Hedging channels you.*

11. *A huge oak offers another Viking sign and a footpath right which you ignore, continuing along the Way to pass a topless railway bridge. Eventually you rise up and over a hump-backed Grantham Canal bridge, the Viking Way continues straight ahead but you turn left at this, Bridge 62, (noting its convenient seat) to follow the towpath along with the canal on your left.*

12. *Soon you pass Woolsthorpe Top Lock (No.18) on your left. (It is being repaired by volunteers from the Grantham Canal Restoration Society . . . Signboard says Grantham Canal 1793 − 1993.)*

   Soon after Lock no.18 make a MENTAL NOTE OF A WHITE-GATED TRACK on the right with an access post at its side.

   The next lock, No. 17, known as Willis's Lock and also being restored, has a lock-keeper's cottage on the opposite bank. Here also, was Woolsthorpe Wharf from whence the ironstone was shipped along the canal to Stanton Ironworks at Ilkeston in Derbyshire.

   You need to go over the bridge by Willis's Lock to desert the canal and pass the Lock-keeper's Cottage to go down its gravelly track which becomes tarmac lane.

LOCK REPAIRS

Once restoration work is finished you WILL be able to cross the canal directly HERE to reach the lane. Until then you are offered short temporary-signed diversions (which may vary as the work progresses) which will achieve the same object by looping you briefly away and back to the canal via a track and under an embankment.

Locks 17 and 18 are close together. If when you reach Lock 18 (with its Lock-keeper's cottage) you do see a 'towpath diversion alongside the embankment' sign you will need to return the short distance to the white gate you noted, pass round the side of it and go along a gravelly track. A high hedge left, low hedge right and power lines ahead to the right, guide you safely to track crossroads where you turn left to go under the embankment, passing the Viking Way sign on your right and heading for the lock-keeper's house ahead.

Soon you see the canal bridge at Willis's Lock (which as already mentioned you would normally cross more directly). When you reach this bridge pass towards it to go up and over it (its sides stunningly frame distant Belvoir Castle) to reach the Lock-keeper's Cottage which you pass to join its tarmac lane.

If the Lock has been repaired and all is back to normal you will be allowed to continue along the towpath to the SECOND of the two locks (No.17, Willis's Lock). In that case you come off the towpath to the right and turn immediately left to pass up and over the canal bridge (No. 61, Woolsthorpe Bridge) to reach and pass the Lock-keeper's Cottage on the opposite bank. Join the cottage's tarmac lane.

In either case, having passed the Lock-keeper's cottage and joined its tarmac lane, you will soon see the 'Rutland Arms' (more commonly known as the 'Dirty Duck'!) nearby below to your right. Continue along this lane, cables cross over and Castle beckons ahead. Ignore the lane to your left where the cables meet but at the country road ahead turn left towards 'Woolsthorpe by Belvoir' sign.

13. *Pavement takes you past Hunt Cottages. Go straight ahead at the crossroads, looking right to see the Belvoir Hunt Stables. Pass the Post Office (or treat yourself to an icecream and a sit − friendly villagers will pass the time of day).*

14. *Continue along to reach the lane from which you emerged earlier, retracing your steps along it and across the fields to turn left at the road and reach the Castle entrance.*

Belvoir Castle

Swannington Village, Incline, Common and Collieries

Outline
Swannington Village and Incline — Snibston No.3 and Calcutta Collieries — Swannington Windmill and Gorse Field Common — Swannington Village.

Summary
A walk along village road, lane and short grassy Incline, past deserted mines, a Church and a Windmill then across ancient Common land to finish at a pub with a playground for children. Welliboots are a good idea, it can be muddy in parts.

The variation eliminates the short steepness of the Incline — but also its enjoyment. Either version can be combined with Route 14 (the Snibston Discovery Park outing). A visit to the fascinating hands-on Science Museum based on the site of the old main Snibston Colliery will add to the understanding of what is seen on this walk.

Attractions
Beginning at the friendly Fountain Inn you walk through a village which in the 17th C. was home to one of the very first Quaker settlements. George Fox, the founder of the movement was arrested here in 1662. The lovely grassy, mercifully short, 1 in 17 gradient of the Incline Plane of the one-time Coleorton Railway can be taken in easy stages, reading the explanatory boards, resting and remembering that wagons used to be hauled up here by the winding engine housed at the top — and that some of the sandstone remaining in the cutting was first quarried in medieval times.

You see what was Snibston No.3 Colliery, investigate the tales of mining hazards as told by gravestones at the Church, then pass the Windmill being restored by enthusiastic volunteers, before crossing ancient common land to see the signs of 13th C. Adit and Bell-pit coalmining now clothed by Mother Nature's camouflage.

The Swannington Heritage Trust, former miners and railwaymen amongst them, are doing wonderful voluntary work all around to preserve, restore and explain this once-busy area. The village post office sells booklets telling more as well as sweets and suchlike!

Route 11

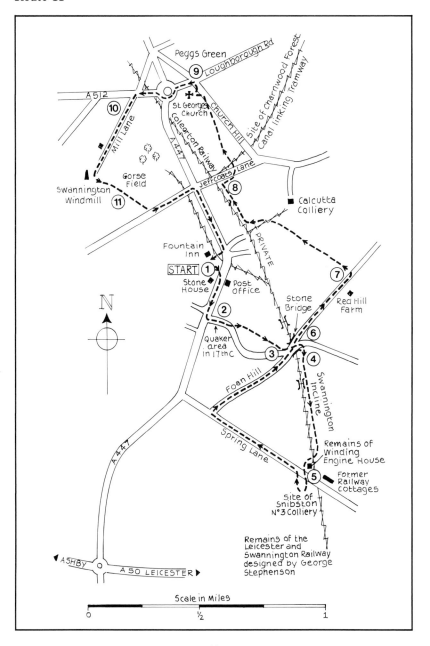

Route 11

Swannington Village, Incline, Common and Collieries   5 miles
or 3¾ miles

Start

From the A.50 between Ashby-de-la-Zouch and Coalville turn right onto the A.447 for Swannington. Pass through the village to reach the Fountain Inn on the left, parking in its car park. The landlord is happy for you to do this . . . and I can recommend his refreshments! GR 415168. Landranger 129 applies.

Route

1. *From the car park walk uphill to the right, passing the Post Office, ignoring the footpath sign on the three-storey stone house on the right and turning left down Church Lane. The 17th C. buildings at the beginning of the lane housed early Quakers.*

2. *Pass down the lane and over the white post-and-rail bridge, then follow the directional arrow of the footpath sign on your left across the field diagonally to reach its right hand corner. (If the going appears very muddy, continue along Church Lane instead to reach Stone Bridge).*

3. *At the field corner climb the wooden steps passing over the stile onto the Incline Plane, turning right along it (left is private). Immediately you will see wooden steps leading to the road and Stone Bridge above you.*

4. *At the blue Heritage Trust Incline sign at Stone Bridge pass through the wooden kissing-gate entrance and down wooden steps into the Incline, heading up towards the notice-board telling about Potato Lane, the ancient green way formerly known as Pit Leys Lane.*
   If however you are taking the short variation (missing out the Incline) you need to keep to the road continuing along it as it changes from Church Lane to Red Hill Lane, following the instructions from 6. and the mention of Stone Bridge.

5. *As you reach the top of the Incline follow the track round left, passing the foundations of the old winding-engine house on your right. As you reach the road (Spring Lane) ahead, pass across it to investigate the remains of Snibston No.3 Colliery before going down Spring Lane to reach and turn along Foan Hill on your right. Continue along it until you reach Stone Bridge once more.*

6. *At Stone Bridge this time continue ahead over it, ignoring the road-junction and the footpath sign to the right.*

7. *Continue on along past Red Hill Farm on the right then take a footpath signed on your left. Below and slightly right lie abandoned Calcutta Colliery, Swannington Common and Gorse Field. Follow the footpath signs and at the bottom of the hill cross the footbridge over the brook, passing up the embankment to join the footpath (which was once part of the Coleorton Railway) as it leads you onto the road ahead (Jeffcoats Lane).*

8. *Turn right along Jeffcoats Lane until you reach the footpath sign to your left which heads you uphill. Follow the hedgeline with the Church above and slightly left, then cross the stile into the road (Church Hill), turning left along its verge briefly to look at Church and gravestones, in particular the tombstone to Harry Clements near the door.*

9. *Come out of the churchyard to pass left along the busy Loughborough Road's pavement for a few yards to reach Pegg's Green island, continuing straight ahead on Loughborough Road for a few more yards to reach the bridleway Mill Lane, turning left along it.*

10. *Pass a house right and go through the wide metal gate alongside to continue straight ahead to Swannington Mill (which is being restored). Immediately after the windmill, to the left, is Gorse Field footpath which you need to follow. This is ancient heathland belonging to the villagers so please treat it with respect. Its humps and hollows confirm that it was the site of 13th C. Adit and Bell-pit coalmining.*

11. *Follow the worn track, keeping its hedgerow to your right. You will soon see a stile in the hedgebottom. Pass over this, and a second, continuing downhill to reach the road and turn left, then right where it meets the main village street. Pass along to reach the Fountain Inn once more.*

Swannington Incline

The Lion Courtyard, Staunton Harold Hall

Route 12   3½ miles
variation 1: 4 miles
variation 2: 2½ miles
variation 3: 2¾ miles

Staunton Harold and Dimminsdale

Outline
Staunton Harold Nurseries – Ferrers Centre – Church – Hall – Dimminsdale – Nurseries

Summary
An easy walk made longer by adding muddy-pathed woodland next to Staunton Harold Hall and its Lake, or shorter by retracing the outward journey at either of two points. The Hall, now a hospice and headquarters of the Ryder-Cheshire mission, contains a Sue Ryder Gift and Coffee Shop and a Cheshire Exhibition.

The Hall's Georgian stableblock is now the popular and attractive Ferrers Centre for Art and Craft, its Church deserves a visit and its parkland adjoins Dimminsdale, a Nature Reserve and Site of Specific Scientific Interest offering traces of Neolithic quarrying and later industries which once funded life at the Hall. Stout footwear is recommended and for safety's sake it is vital to keep to the footpath in Dimminsdale. Dogs must be on a lead and please go quietly, the occasional deer seeks sanctuary here.

Both the Ferrers Centre and the Nurseries offer delicious home-made refreshments.

Attractions
Pevsner wrote 'for position, Staunton Harold, the house and the chapel are unsurpassed in the country'. Today you are free to enjoy private parkland, investigate a rare 1650's Church, feed wildfowl by an 18th C. lake and take tea in the 18th C. Hall, its swallow-studded suntrap stableyard or the Nurseries.

Watch cabinet and guitar makers and potters at work (some using estate-grown wood), visit the Sue Ryder gift shop and another run by enterprising villagers to fund the village school they saved, bought and now manage themselves; last but definitely not least, enjoy the current displays in the wonderfully restored Craft-Council-selected Ferrers Gallery.

The box-pewed, panelled and naive-painted Church was built by the staunch Royalist, Sir Robert Shirley, who in 1653 ended up in the Tower for his pains. Cromwell already suspected him of plotting to restore the monarchy so his building of a forbidden Church in defiance of Cromwell was foolhardy or brave! Sir Robert died in the Tower in 1656 at the age of 28 . . . his Church survived despite being built under Cromwell's very nose!

Another Shirley, Laurence, Earl of Ferrers, knew the Tower – he was one of the last peers to be hanged there. Overfond of drink, he cruelly ill-treated his wife who

·

obtained a divorce. John Johnson, luckless Steward of the Shirley estate, had to pay her awarded settlement from estate rents. This did not please the Earl who, in a fit of temper, shot Johnson, then unsuccessfully defended himself by conducting his own trial and pleading insanity! His body was eventually brought back from London and lies at Staunton Harold.

Once part of the estate, Dimminsdale Nature Reserve is now an S.S.S.I. having outlived limestone quarrying from the 13th C. onwards, lead-mining in the 1600's, the working of fiery kilns producing lime, the building and operating of a tramway to transport burnt lime in the 1800's, the operation of the cottage laundry established in 1898 to wash the Hall's dirty linen, the collapse of the mine due to illegal quarrying around 1850 and, more recently, the creation of nearby Staunton Harold Reservoir.

Mother Nature has her own way with man-inflicted wounds. She has clothed the area so beautifully that it has become a haven for flora and fauna. Visit in February and it is dressed in a profusion of snowdrops. Wonderfully peaceful now, it is hard to believe that for centuries it was a noisy, smelly, fiery foretaste of hell for those who worked here.

Staunton Harold Church

Route 12

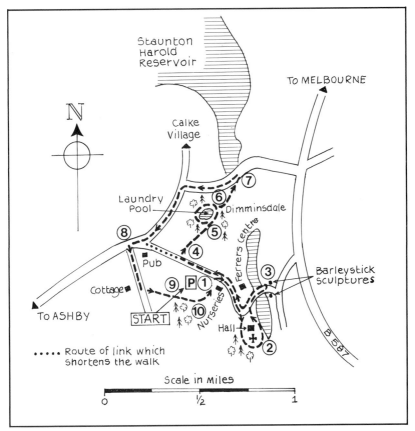

Staunton Harold Reservoir

TO MELBOURNE

N

Calke Village

Laundry Pool

Dimminsdale

⑦

⑥

⑧

⑤

④

Ferrers Centre

Pub

③

Barleystick sculptures

Cottage

⑨ P ①

Nurseries

Hall

②

TO ASHBY

START

⑩

B 587

..... Route of link which shortens the walk

Scale in miles

0   ½   1

Route 12

Staunton Harold and Dimminsdale

3½ miles
variations: by adding woodland: 4 miles
by returning from Dimminsdale: 2½ miles
by returning along estate drive: 2¾ miles

Start

From Ashby-de-la-Zouch take the A.453 to Lount (signposted Breedon, Castle Donington and Nottingham). At Lount turn left onto the B.587 then left into Staunton Harold Grounds, following brown signs. Park behind the Nurseries, following more signs. GR 379209 Landranger Map 128 applies.

Route

1. *From the Nurseries, pass the Ferrers Centre for Arts and Crafts to take the signposted route to 'Church and Car Park', soon turning off left to sweep round the lion-topped south front, noticing the small gravestone to 'Bogie'. Continue along the tree-lined Walk as it brings you lakewards, then swing left to go through the narrow stone archway to the Church.*

    Several footbridges into the woodland on the right offer paths to explore. Remembering that a narrow (inaccessible from the wood) estate track lies beyond the far outside edge of the wood and the lake lies at the bottom side of the wood, any path will eventually lead you back onto grass by Hall and Church.

2. *On leaving the Church head straight for the Hall, passing up left to walk along the side containing the entrance to the Cheshire Exhibition and toilets. The Sue Ryder Coffee and Gift Shop is signed on the next side.*

3. *Investigate the barleystick entrance gate sculptures by the lake then return upwards to retrace your steps past the Ferrers Centre. Continue along the state drive past Nurseries and farmhouses and pass downhill.*

4. *At the yellowtopped post on a slight ridge right, turn right to follow the ridge to another marked post whose direction sign you follow along the grassy track, hugging tall hawthorn-hedged right boundary.*

5. *Pass over signed, stiled fencing into woodland, continuing straight ahead. Follow arrow direction, slightly left, keeping to woodland path. At next waymark pass over stile and turn right uphill towards woodland edge. You are now in Dimminsdale Nature Reserve, owned by Severn Trent Water Authority, managed by Leicestershire and Rutland Trust for Nature Conservation and a 'Site of Special Scientific Interest'. Please treat it respectfully. FOR SAFETY'S SAKE keep to the footpath, dogs must be on lead.*

71

The following instructions will help you keep to the official footpath round the Reserve:

Follow as the path swings round woodland edge and up wired brick and wood steps, keeping to path, ignoring all worn trods off. Below left is Laundry Pool and the remains of a quarry. Follow path down round the quarry edges, down steps to admire the pool from its bank before crossing the footbridge right and second one again to your right.

Pass up to noticeboard in trees on right, this path continues to the road. You return here later but for now observe the overgrown remains of limestone kilns then return down steps and along footpath to the right (once the route of the Ashby-Ticknall tramway which transported lime and lead produced here).

Follow the path with brook left and waterfilled neolithic quarries right. With barbed-wire fencing right and wide gate ahead pathway leads you round left and down steps.

Follow path over footbridge, then uphill to more steps (all made by hardworking L.R.T.N.C. volunteers). As you climb steps you see the stile over which you entered Dimminsdale.

Retrace your outward path from this point to shorten your walk and return to Staunton Harold Hall, thus avoiding a stretch of pavementless road.

To continue main walk, follow footpath round once more to regain poolside, turning right up steps to pass noticeboard and continue out to reach road.

6. *At the road you need to turn left, but first go right briefly to bend in road for views of Staunton Harold Reservoir.*

7. *Return along pavementless road, passing exit from Dimminsdale and continuing uphill to 'T' junction signed 'Calke Village' right and 'Ashby' left. Turn towards Ashby, passing up, then down to round the bend at bottom of hill. Ignore sign for Staunton Harold and pass Saracen's Head on left to reach bridleway sign left a few yards further on.*

    Should you wish to shorten your walk or take advantage of tarmac you can however turn left at the sign for Staunton Harold, following pot-holed drive.

8. *To continue main walk turn left along bridleway, passing up incline to reach much-bridged cottage right. Opposite it left is yellow waymarked stile over which you pass, continuing ahead. Keep to right boundary to pass around brick stable and barn and go through adjacent gates. Continue straight ahead past solitary oak right.*

9. *Pass under telegraph wires, hold to left to reach wood corner ahead where you will see waymarked post and stile. Pass over following direction sign up slope. Distant left hedgeline gives glimpses of your outward estate-road route.*

10. *Pass hawthorned dewpond and go gently upwards to next waymarked post at woodland edge. Cross stile into next field and head towards waymarked stile at wood edge, Nursery and brick-and-white cottage lie beyond.*

Pass over stile to reach next waymarked post at edge of your car park. For easiest line follow hedgeside until you meet grasstrack by an oak tree, it will take you to waymark and carpark.

Staunton Harold Church

Bradgate Park

Outline
Cock Glade Gates − Tyburn − War Memorial − Old John − Cropston Reservoir − Bradgate Ruins − Cock Glade Gates

Summary
An easy 'guided tour' of perhaps Leicestershire's most popular leisure-time venue. Childhood home of Lady Jane Grey, the nine-day Queen of England, Bradgate's hills are grassy-tracked and gentle and its tarmac drive makes for easy walking. There is a Visitors' Centre, gift shop and toilets and ample parking for which you are asked to donate 50p. Several cafes and a garden centre also welcome children almost opposite the Church (which has an unusual 'apprentice piece', an alphabet carved in local slate). Further along the village road are several pubs.

Attractions
Bradgate's brackened hills, red and fallow deer roaming freely (if shyly) amongst visitors, history and ruins offer something for everyone. Huge wrought iron 'Cock Glade Gates' (so-called because woodcocks roosted at this point) welcome you. Shortly thereafter you pass Tyburn Spinney where Bradgate's aged and infirm hunting hounds were hanged (considered the most humane treatment at the time).

Most of the spinneys were planted in the 1800's for shooting but Bradgate's scenery offers an idea of what the landscape elsewhere would have been like before widespread clearance for farming . . . but with less bracken and more oak, hazel, birch and rowan trees.

Over the centuries Bradgate has been grazed by horses, cattle, sheep and rabbits as well as deer, thus allowing the bracken to proliferate. So much so it became an important crop for the locals, being burnt from midsummer on by the neighbourhood poor who made the ashes into balls sold to make lye for clothes washing. They also collected acorns to sell as pig-feed, gorse as firewood and horsechestnuts as food.

Bradgate had its poachers, one in the 1800's being caught feeding currants soaked in whisky to the pheasants. It was very easy to pick up drunken pheasants and store them in a convenient hollow oak!

When you see 'Old John', the tankard-shaped tower, remember the old miller whose name it bears. He was, reputedly, very fond of his ale. At a bonfire for the coming-of-age party of the Earl of Stamford's son he was accidentally hit on the head by a falling, burning log and the family created the tower in 1786 in his memory. Remember, too, the men of the Leicestershire Yeomanry who died in the First World War when you see their tall, slim Memorial close by 'Old John'.

Imagine the area as it would have been earlier when horse − and hound − races were held around the miller's tower with the nobility using it as a grandstand. Originally the site, of course, held a windmill.

Cropston Reservoir offers waterfowl as you pass. Built in 1860, it swallowed up twelve farms and the Head Keeper's house, the Stables and Kennels. Nearby is the Visitors' Centre and thereafter the spectacular ruin of the brick mansion begun by Thomas Grey, first Marquess of Dorset in 1490. It was finished by the second Marquess, grandfather of Lady Jane Grey, nine-day-Queen, who grew up at Bradgate only to be beheaded in 1554. Today's old oaks which edge the drive are said to have had *their* heads chopped off by the locals of the time in sympathy, though pollarding of oaks was common in parkland of the period.

Outside Lady Jane's old home is another old oak under which Queen Adelaide, widow of William lV picnicked in 1842, eating 'venison which was good, so were the trout and not least the crayfish . . . the trout being literally made to leap out of the water into the frying pan'. The little River Lyn from whence they leapt accompanies you as you wend your way out of this fascinating backwater.

The Park, already enclosed by 1247, has never been cultivated or landscaped and thus offers an almost unique example of how a medieval hunting park would have looked. It was given to the people of Leicester for their enjoyment in 1928.

Peacock by Bradgate Ruins

75

Route 13

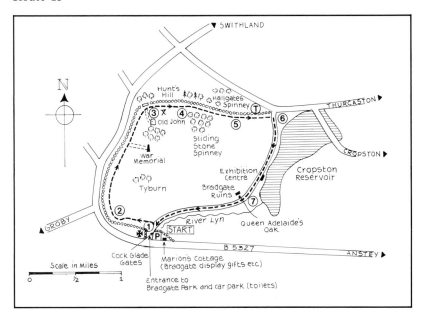

Route 13

Bradgate Park   5 miles

Start

Newtown Linford Car Park. Newtown Linford lies 6 miles NW of Leicester on the B.5327. Turn right by the village Church and into the Car Park. Enter the Park itself through the tall wooden kissing-gate at the right of the wrought-iron Cock Glade Gates. GR 523098. Landranger Map 129 applies.

Note that paths in Bradgate are alternated from time to time to reduce erosion, but the general direction remains the same.

Route

1. *Enter the Park at the tall wooden kissing-gate and turn left immediately to follow the stony path uphill, deserting the main drive. Continue uphill, passing through stonewall opening with its yellow-topped post. Where the bridleway sweeps right you continue to hug stone wall to your left on narrower track.*

2. *Tyburn Spinney lies ahead and you pass two more wooden gates to the Park. Keep to left hand path as it rejoins bridleway, keeping stone wall left, continuing to climb. War Memorial lies right, detour to inspect it then return to continue uphill.*

3. *At the top you will see wooden 'Hunts Hill' Gate and to your right an ancient track winding up from it to 'Old John'. This area is believed to have been an important Saxon (or even Druidic) meeting place. Divert to inspect 'Old John', returning to pass the tall kissing-gate entrance and nearby picnic bench and continue to follow the stonewall left as it passes downhill.*

4. *Pass over small wooden footbridge, go past another kissing-gate left, waterworks also lie left. A spinney lies right as you link briefly with tarmac driveway which swings round from your right. An underground reservoir lies gravel-topped right. Where tarmac ends continue ahead with stone wall and woodland left.*

5. *Crest the rise, ahead lies Cropston Reservoir and nearer, a convenient seat. Pass downhill towards reservoir with your faithful left hand wall. At yellow-marked gate turn left along wide track, going left alongside stone wall with car park and toilets beyond.*

6. *This is 'Hallgates' entrance where you turn right along the tarmac drive with Reservoir left. Look for 'wildfowl-watching' windows and seats in stone wall boundary left. Next pass (or investigate) the Visitors' Centre left before reaching Queen Adelaide's Oak, Bradgate ruins, surviving chapel and prospecting peacocks to the right.*

7. *After exploring ruins return to tarmac drive, it will lead you alongside the companionable River Lyn back to Cock Glade Gates.*

Snibston Discovery Park and
Snibston Grange Nature Reserve

Outline
Exhibition Hall — Grange Nature Reserve — Exhibition Hall

Summary
This easy stroll begins at a new internationally acclaimed 'hands-on' science discovery park and exhibition hall and takes you through its all-weather —pathed pleasant countryside setting (some of it , unbelievedly, former colliery spoil area) and alongside a golf driving range to explore the nature reserve of nearby Snibston Grange and its ponds. The Grange and its lodge have long gone but its arboretum welcomes you and your return route takes you atop a green and grassy trail offering splendid views on all sides.

Access is free, so is car parking and entrance to the large reception foyer of the Exhibition Hall with its refreshment area, toilets, shop and tourist information centre. I recommend that you extend your visit to include a visit to the Exhibition Hall proper and the Colliery Trail. Admission is £4 for adults, £2.75 for children and senior citizens, etc; or buy a family ticket for £10. The Colliery Tour costs £1 for adults, 50 pence children, under-fives free. Tickets are valid all day and the facilities can be visited in any order and frequency. They are open year-round but telephone 01530 813256 for seasonal variations in opening hours.

Attractions
This is a very easy walk, with wet weather facilities close at hand in the shape of the Exhibition Hall and huge science and industry Museum. The free outdoor facilities include Snibston Grange Nature Reserve with its mature trees and fishing ponds and its explanatory boards — the sharp-eyed may spot a rare Short-eared Owl amongst many other species.

Snibston was the site of George and Robert Stephenson's first mine shaft sunk in 1832 but the area had already known mining in medieval times and an exhibition offers artifacts from 1450's deep shaft mining at nearby Coleorton as well as a taste of the dreadful conditions endured by the men, women and children who worked below ground. A visit here will enhance understanding of the sights to be seen on Route 11.

Snibston also has a sculpture trail, a wheelwright's workshop, a sawmill, a blacksmith's shop and an indoor picnic area. Soon to be opened are a site railway, a coal mine simulation and a model farm.

Probably the children's favourite will be the Science Alive! Gallery where you and they can play with lightning, walk through a tornado, launch a hot air balloon or cycle with a skeleton, and much, much more! The outdoor science playground has fifteen more big experiments.

Indoor galleries include Textiles, Fashion and Engineering (where you can test your strength against a system of pulleys) . . . in fact the choice is so wide you'll pray for it to rain!

Colliery Trail, Snibston Discovery Park

Route 14

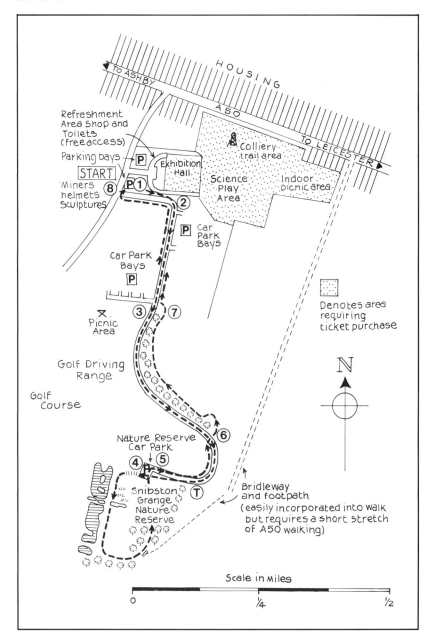

Route 14

Snibston Discovery Park and   **2 miles**
Snibston Grange Nature Reserve

Start

From Leicester take the A50 to Coalville where Snibston Discovery Park lies on the Ashby Road . It is well sign-posted from all directions, large brown and white signs). Park in the bays in front of the Exhibition Hall or further parking bays beyond. (GR 417147) Landranger Map 129 applies.

Route

1. *From the car park head towards the Exhibition Hall entrance doors, then pass around outside the right hand side of the Hall towards tall metal emergency access gates, thus putting the huge crane 'Bennie' and the Hall on your immediate left and following the direction of a nature trail and a car park sign.*

2. *Pass up the gravelly wooden-fenced path towards the tarmac drive. The children's Science Playground lies below left and where the path reaches the road turn slightly right, then immediately left following the direction of the nature trail and car park sign.*

3. *Pass more car park bays left and right, continuing uphill with the tarmac road, later passing the golf driving range on the right as you begin to bear downhill and right following the direction of the nature trail and fishing pond sign. Cabin toilets are available to your left and just beyond them you can take a stile over fencing to your left to enter the corner of the woodland and desert the road, joining the woodland footpath to the right. It will take you round the edge of the wood briefly, bringing you to the nature trail car park. However it is easier to remain on the tarmac drive for the few yards it takes to reach the car park with its large green nature trail signboard.*

4. *Either way, at the green signboard pass down the wooden-fenced and wooden-edged steps towards the pools below, noting the signs telling you the tree species. Where you reach the main pool with its 'Danger Deep Water No Swimming' sign turn left along the gravel track to pass it and the other pools, eventually swinging left with the path towards trees once more. Pass the convenient seat and head upwards into the trees as you sweep round past the 'Atlas Cedar' and soon swing right, passing another seat in this attractive mature woodland.*

5. *When the path returns you to the Nature Reserve car park once more turn right to return up the tarmac drive towards the toilet cabins whence you came.*

6. *As you reach the bend in the road with the golf course immediately left and a short wide gravelly track right, pass up its adjacent steep cut-grass trail. Newly set trees will be to your left. Follow the track as it rises sharply and shortly up this former slag heap which offers a panoramic route back to the museum, making its initial short climb well worthwhile . . . though you can continue along the accompanying tarmac drive below if steepness is a deterrent.*

7. *The trail offers the golf driving range below left and a sports field to the right as well as distant views of the Charnwood hills and beyond. Eventually at a wide opening on your left − sporting short wooden posts and a blue car park arch opposite − the cut grass trail ends so turn left to go down to the tarmac drive below. Turn right along it to return downwards to the car park and Hall entrance.*

8. *This time though, I suggest you ignore the wooden fenced gravelly track dropping directly down to the Hall. Instead go down the drive to reach its tiny 'T' junction where you can admire the miner's helmet sculptures before returning to the adjacent car park outside the Hall entrance.*

Burrough Hill Iron Age Hillfort

Outline
Burrough Hill Country Park — Hillfort Entrance and Camp — Toposcope —
Burrough Hill Covert — Hillfort Entrance — Country Park car park.

Summary
Easy walking, one short steep downward scramble and one gentle climb, both of
which can be eliminated if you choose to take your own line and wander at will (but
respecting boundary markers which are small white figures over-striped with red).
This ancient hillfort site offers grassy peacefulness roughly seven hundred feet above
sea-level and 82 acres of Country Park . . . dogs must be on a lead for today's
inhabitants are sheep! Stout footwear should suffice, but some areas can be muddy.

Attractions
This is a walk with few signs of civilisation . . . hence the peacefulness! A protected
ancient monument, its huge shallow grassy bowl offers children freedom to romp
whilst adults can watch from the rim and conjure up images of past inhabitants and
happenings since the last few centuries B.C. Earliest finds date from around 2,000
years ago when it was almost certainly built as a refuge for locals against marauding
neighbouring tribes. The earthen rampart banks would probably have been topped by
a timber palisade, with strong gates closing off the entrance.

Much later, 1540, records show that each Whitsun people came here to run,
wrestle, dance, shoot, etc., in its convenient 'arena' which later again, in the 1800's,
was used for horse-racing events organised by the Melton Hunt.

The walk also offers the opportunity to add the very attractive permissive Dalby
Hills Path, one and a quarter miles long, but don't forget you then need to return along
it to the hillfort. The Dalby Hills Path is closed for a few days each year but I
understand a decision has been made to close only on Thursdays in the shooting season
(which is roughly September to February).

The signboard at its beginning will alert you if it should prove to be shut, otherwise
the footpath's grey waymarkers guide you onwards when the path is open.

This is one walk with no access to refreshments, but you can make your visit as
long or as short as you wish, there are plenty of suitable picnic points and Oakham
is not far by road and offers much in the way of refreshment and interest. In fact the
combination of Route 4 (an exploration of Oakham and the 'bustle' of a market town)
with the peaceful top-of-the-world spaciousness of this, Burrough Hill, makes for an
interesting day!

Parking is 50p., pay and display machine and toilets are close by, though the latter
may not be open in winter. Please remember that Burrough Hill is a protected ancient
monument and treat it with respect.

Route 15

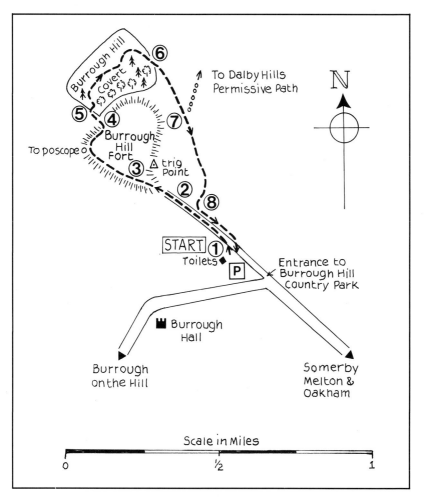

Fox

Route 15

Burrough Hill Iron Age Hillfort   2 miles, variation: 4½ miles

Start

From Leicester head for Melton Mowbray via the A.607, there taking the A606 towards Oakham, eventually turning right towards Somerby. The Hillfort lies beyond the village of Somerby on the road to Burrough-on-the-Hill. Access to Burrough Hill Country Park and the fort is on a signposted bend and is open in daylight hours throughout the year. Park in the car park. GR 767116. Landranger Map 139 applies.

Route

1. *From the Car Park, with the toilets on your left and the entrance behind you, follow the wide cream gravel track to the wooden gate with its sign 'Car Park 50p.', passing through and continuing ahead. Ignore footpath signs to right and left, progressing to the Country Park notice board up ahead.*

2. *At the board ignore the footpath to the right and enter the field through a handgate to pass gently upwards in the direction of the green sign 'Burrough Hill Camp'. The triangular stone of the trig point lies right as you head towards the gap in the green ramparts marking the entrance to the old fort (which would once have had stout wooden gates, just as the green ramparts would have been wooden-palisaded.)*

3. *Walk left atop the fortification ridge on your left, it will lead you round to the toposcope where you can pick out many landmarks. Next bear round right atop the ramparts to draw level with the woodland, Burrough Hill Covert, below on your left.*

4. *Once level with the edge of the wood, desert the ramparts by passing left down their steepness to reach a stile on the woodland edge fencing to your right. Small signs tell you that this covert is open to the public.*

5. *Pass over the stile into the woodland and follow the narrow worn path downhill to your left to reach the bottom where an enormous beech tree beckons. Turn right at this low point to follow the wider grassy track to your right through the wood.*

6. *Soon after passing a convenient seat on your left follow the now narrow path round to come out of the wood at more wooden fencing with a stile. Next join the farm track emerging from a double-gated wooden farm pen in the fencing on your left, turning right along the track, it will guide you gently uphill towards a yellow-topped post.*

7. At the post, ignore its path to the left but join its path to the right, continuing to pass upwards.

    However, should you wish to extend your walk by taking the 'Dalby Hills Footpath' (a mile and a quarter long) and then returning to this point, a turn left along the footpath at the post will deliver you to the start of the Dalby Hills Footpath.

    To continue your exploration of the Burrough Hill site, continue upwards and across the traces of ridge and furrow (with the trig point to your right) and soon you will see distantly ahead the Iron Age Camp's noticeboard by a group of shrubby trees.

8. Come out at the handgate by the noticeboard to rejoin the cream track and reach the car park by turning left along it.

Hawthorn on Burrough Hill Ramparts

Moira Furnace

Outline
Moira Furnace and Craft Workshops − Ashby Canal − Lime kilns − Engine House Cottage − Ashby and Nuneaton Joint Railway − Ashby Road − Children's Play Area and Moira Furnace.

Summary
An easy, short walk incorporating part of the Ashby Wolds Heritage Trail (once part of the Ashby and Nuneaton Joint Railway); one of our best preserved furnaces dating from the Napoleonic Wars and part of an Industrial History Trail and a tiny section of the towpath of the former Ashby Canal, with a children's recreation ground thrown in for good measure.

Attractions
Beginning with the beautifully restored and maintained Moira Furnace and its attendant craft shops housing a blacksmith, a carpenter and carver, a model aircraft maker, a saddler and a potter, this is a walk of contrasts. There is industrial heritage a-plenty, all kindly mellowed by nature aided by today's citizens. It is hard to realise that from blast furnace to lime kilns, all owe their presence here to the existence of coal in the Ashby Wolds.

The furnace was loaded from the top with coal and ironstone and the fire fed by blasts of air from a Newcomen steam engine. (The Ashby Wolds coal deposits contained iron ore, hence the building of the furnace to separate it from the coal). The molten metal moved downwards at around 1200 degrees C. to be run off into sand beds. When the foundry ceased operations in the mid-eighteen hundreds the furnace was converted into dwellings.

The canal was built between 1794 and 1804 to take coal to distant cities such as London and Oxford. In use until the 1940's, it was abandoned due to subsidence problems and then filled in. The railway sidings have become a nature reserve and the whole area is now wonderfully peaceful but the huge wheel and its sculpture remember and remind us of the miners, furnaceworkers and railwaymen who spent their lives − or gave their lives − in what must have been a dusty, noisy, hell on earth.

With friendly craftspeople working by the furnace, trail extensions planned etc., all that is needed now is a source of home-made refreshments on site. However, the Engine Pub at nearby Donisthorpe more than compensates for that lack and children are welcome. Nearer to the Furnace, the Navigation Inn on the Ashby Road still offers refreshment to today's traveller as it once did to the canal boatmen − it lies next to the line of the old canal.

STOP PRESS: Since writing the above it has been announced that the new National Forest is to have a Visitor Centre at Moira Furnace, plus a Forest Resource Trail and Pathway.

Route 16

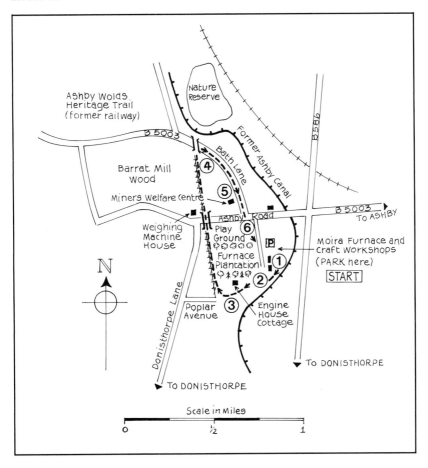

Route 16

Moira Furnace   2 miles

Start

From Leicester take the A.50 to Ashby. Moira Furnace is approximately three miles from Ashby de la Zouch on the B5003 and is signposted to the left on the way out of the village of Moira. Park in the Furnace car park. GR 314152. Landranger Map 128 applies.

I recommend that you pick up a Moira Trail leaflet (10p.) and an Ashby Wolds Heritage Trail leaflet (15p.) from a Tourist Information Centre or Moira Post Office prior to the walk. You can then walk either trail in full or ensure that you see everything of interest to you.

Route

1. Inspect the craft courtyard and the Furnace, making full use of the excellent signboards before passing up steps to view the canal bed and then turn right along what was its towpath, leaving the Furnace behind, keeping the empty canal to your left and passing under the archways.

2. Where the canal has been filled in you will see a yellow signpost. Follow the footpath until you reach new wooden fencing ahead with a yellow-signed gap for you to pass onto grassed-over wasteland. Go through the gap and turn immediately right, keeping the fencing on your right and following it along to reach the end of telegraph wires and a gap in the new fencing which allows you to change sides.

3. Pass through the gap to turn left and reach the wooden steps of an old pedestrian way which crossed what was the railway track. You will see a sign saying 'Moira Trail No. 11'. Turn right here along this, the signed 'Ashby Heritage Trail' and 'Moira to Measham Railway Line', reading all the explanatory signs as you go. Cottages and a lane lie immediately below to your right and soon you pass over a bridge.

4. When you reach wooden steps down to the road at a further bridge, desert the railway and pass down to the road where you turn right to head along the pavement. Playground equipment sparkles distantly right, close by the Furnace and Furnace Wood.

5. Pass the Miners Welfare Club on the right with an adjacent memorial. Shortly thereafter there is a footpath sign on your right which will lead you eventually to the Furnace. However it is currently closed whilst alterations are completed so continue along the road for this last short stretch to reach the huge wheel by the Furnace Museum entrance.

6. *Cross the road to reach the wheel and inspect it and the sculpted pictures below — and their explanation on the reverse, then head for the children's playground where you bear left to join the main track, turning right along it to reach the Furnace area and the car park.*

Moira Furnace, Ashby Wolds

Stable Block Tower, Gumley Hall (Route 9)

Useful information

Routes in Order of Difficulty

Easy walks, flat throughout:

Route 1   Breedon-on-the-Hill (By parking and commencing at the Church with the driver returning there at the end of the walk to collect the car and pick up the less energetic at the Memorial or Garden Centre below). Includes gentle downhill walking.

Route 3   Zouch Cut

Route 4   A Trip Around Oakham

Route 12   Staunton Harold (omit Dimminsdale)

Route 13   Bradgate Park (by keeping to the main drive or paths close by rather than following the perimeter)

Route 15   Burrough Hill Iron Age Fort (by omitting woodland leg)

Less easygoing walks, a few gentle gradients or rough patches:

Route 2   Bosworth Battlefield

Route 5   Brooksby, Hoby and Rotherby

Route 7   Hambleton and Rutland Water

Route 9   Foxton Locks, Foxton and Gumley

Route 10   Belvoir Castle and Woolsthorpe-by-Belvoir

Route 12   Staunton Harold and Dimminsdale

Route 13   Bradgate Park

Route 14   Snibston Discovery Park

Route 15   Burrough Hill Iron Age Fort

Route 16   Moira Furnace

More strenuous walks involving steepish gradients and/or some rough going:

Route 1   Breedon-on-the-Hill

Route 6   Broombriggs and Woodhouse Eaves

Route 8   Mount St. Bernard Abbey and Blackbrook

Most suitable walks for 'beginning tinies' in order of tiny child appeal:

Route 12   Staunton Harold minus Dimminsdale has lake with ducks to watch and feed, small wood to explore, grassy areas, craft centre, working craftsmen making mechanical toys, dolls, etc., shops, home-made refreshments, all within easy reach

Route 2   Bosworth Battlefield has Exhibition Centre with life-size models, film of battle, shop, home made refreshments and grassy spaces

Route 4   Oakham has grassy play area, roundabout, etc., plus castle and museum , shops, cafes all close by and you can eliminate the final leg

Route 3   Zouch has ducks to feed, a childrens' playground and village shop halfway, narrowboats to see both en-route and at the waterside pub at the end of what, for tinies, will be a long way and a big achievement!

Walks where less active 'golden-oldies' can sit in car or out with plenty to interest them whilst you walk:

Route 12   Staunton Harold has lots happening in a small area, seats everywhere, toilets and refreshments, all close to the car park

Route 3   Bosworth Battlefield, exhibition, refreshments, toilets, shop, seats, etc., all at hand

Route 14   Snibston Discovery Park has museum, shop, cafe, toilets and car park all close

The following information is given as a guide only. Bus routes, operators, times of opening etc., are prone to change from time to time so telephone numbers are provided with the recommendation that you check details before setting out on any expedition.

Bus Operators
Telephone BUSLINE on 01162 511411 when planning your outing or obtain the 'Guide to Public Transport in Leicestershire' available from Leicestershire Tourism on 01162 657039.

The following are telephone numbers of some of the coach companies serving the vicinity of the various walks, though since operators may change at short notice Busline is your best source. Please note the information about the forthcoming changes in telephone numbers at the beginning of this book (currently page 7). If in difficulty try Directory Enquiries on 192.

NEJ Coach Travel (Melton area) 01162 762648
Paul James Coaches (Heather, Ashby area) 01664 424474
Paul Winson Coaches (Loughborough, Derby area) 01509 232354
T. H. Skinner and Son (Oakham, Leicester) 01476 860232
Stevensons of Uttoxeter (Loughborough, Coalville) 01283 44662
United Counties (Market Harborough area) 01604 702112
Woods (Market Harborough area) 01162 786374

Cycle hire is available at Whitwell and Normanton for the area around Rutland Water: 01780 86705 or 01780 720513

Tourist Information Centres
Leicester 2-6 St. Martin's Walk, 01162 511300
Ashby de la Zouch Library, Museum, 01530 411767
Loughborough John Storer House 01509 230131
Battlefield Centre, Bosworth (summer only) 01455 292239
Market Harborough, Pen Lloyd Library, Adam and Eve St. 01858 462649
Melton Mowbray Melton Carnegie Museum, Thorpe End. 01664 69946
Oakham Library, Catmos St. 01572 724329

Wet weather alternatives:

Museums
Ashby, North Street. 01503 560090. Small local museum. Exhibits include large model of Ashby Castle and reconstructed turn of century shop.
Donington Castle Donington (on A453 not far from Breedon) 01332 801140. World's largest collection of single seater racing cars, souvenir shop and cafeteria.
Snibston Not to be missed hands-on Science and Industry Museum 01530 510851
Manor House, Donington-le-Heath. Another must, a fine medieval manor house restored as a period house. Small but it has home made food in its barn . . . closes for the winter, sadly. 01530 31259. Close to Snibston.
Jewry Wall, Museum of Leicestershire Archaeology and Roman Baths site plus 2nd C. massive wall. Leicester centre. 01162 544766
John Doran Gas Museum, Aylestone Road, Leicester, only gas museum regularly open in the country. 01162 535506
Leicestershire Museum and Art Gallery, Rutland, geology and history, dinosaur, ancient Egypt, art and ceramics. New Walk, Leicester. 01162 554100
Leicestershire Museum of Technology, Corporation Road, Abbey Lane, Leicester. Housed in former pumping station, original beam engines, transport, knitting 01162 661330
Newarke Houses Museum, Leicester centre. Leicestershire social history from AD 1500 including street scene. 01162 554100

Wygston's House Museum of Costume, Leicester centre. Important late medieval building full of costumes and textiles. 01162 554100.
Great Central Railway Museum, Loughborough. Museum, refreshment room, shop, steam train rides. 01509 230726, for opening times etc. (usually Weds., Sat., Sun.).
Bellfoundry Museum, Freehold St., Loughborough. All aspects of bellfounding from early times, well equipped working bellfoundry. 01509 233414.
Harborough Museum, Council Offices, Market Harborough. Local museum. 01858 32468
Rutland County Museum, Catmos Street, Oakham. Superb, friendly local rural museum in old cavalry riding school. 01572 723654

East Midlands International Airport Aeropark, aircraft exhibits, viewing mound, play area and picnic tables with, indoors, a Visitor Centre portraying history and technology of flight, books, models, pictures, etc.

Garden Centres, Craft Centres, Covered Markets, etc.
Priory Nurseries, Ashby Road, Breedon on the Hill 01332 862406. Garden Centre, Pick Your Own, Refreshments, shops, events.
Ferrers Craft Centre and Gallery, Staunton Harold. Pottery, woodworking, weaving etc., tea shop, gallery. Well worth a visit, garden centre and more shops adjacent. Exhibitions. 01332 863337.
Lucas Garden Centre Newton Lane, Wigston Magna 01162 883375 stable yard craft shops and tea room.
Whitemoors Craft Centre, Shenton, near Bosworth Battlefield. Craft and antique centre, restored barns, tea shop. 01455 212250
Wistow Garden Centre, south east of Leicester, garden centre with tea shop, model village and craft gallery. 01162 592009
Ashby Victorian indoor market adjacent to Town Hall—different days, different objects, open seven days a week, cafeteria.
Market Harborough has an indoor market Tues, Fri and Sat.

Sports and Leisure Centres
Charnwood, Brown's Lane, Loughborough 01509 611080
Granby Halls, Aylestone Road, Leicester 01162 552644
Harborough, Northampton Road 01858 410115
Hood Park, Ashby , North Street 01503 412181
Melton College Leisure Centre, Asfordby Road 01664 69280

Historic Buildings, Castles, etc.
Ashby Castle, Ashby-de-la Zouch centre. Remains of Norman manor-become-castle, 01530 413343.
Belvoir Castle, near Grantham. Superb seat of the Duke of Rutland, pictures, state rooms, museum of the Lancers. Location of films 'Little Lord Fauntleroy' and 'Young Sherlock Holmes', cafeteria. 01476 870262.
Bradgate House, Bradgate Park, Newtown Linford 01162 362713
Kirby Muxloe Castle, 01162 386886, ruined fortified manor house with moat.
Oakham Castle, 01572 723654, part of late 12 C. manor house with unique collection of horseshoes left by Royal and noble visitors.
The Old Rectory, Rectory Place, Loughborough, 01509 214995, ancient building and local archaeological museum

Farm Centres
Farmworld, Stoughton Farm Park Farmworld, Gartree Road, Oadby, 3 miles from Leicester, Shire horses, cart rides, working dairy farmyard and milking parlour, children's farmyard and playgrounds picnic areas, exhibitions and crafts, refreshments and shop. 01162 710355.
Our Little Farm. Small farm centre in Vale of Belvoir. Victorian farm buildings, nature trail, abandoned canal and railway, tearoom and gift shop. 01949 60349.
Stonehurst Farm, Loughborough Road, Mountsorrel, Farm Trail and 'Cuddle Corner', motor and motorbike museum, farm machinery and blacksmith's forge, homemade refreshments and farm shop. 01509 413216.

Background Reading on the Area
Leicestershire and Rutland, Nikolaus Pevsner Penguin Books
Charnwood Forest, A Changing Landscape, A. E. Squires and others, Sycamore Press
The Story of Melton Mowbray, Philip E. Hunt, Leics. Libraries
The Folklore of Leics. and Rutland, Roy Palmer, Sycamore Press
An Exploration of the Leicester Navigation, Brian C. J. Williams, Leic. Navigation 200 Group
A History of Leics. and Rutland, Roy Millward, Phillimore
Place Names of Leicestershire and Rutland, Jill Bourne, Leics. Libraries
The Coritani, Malcolm Todd, Alan Sutton
The Melton to Oakham Canal, David Tew, Sycamore Press
Wind and Watermills of Rutland, David Henry, Spiegl Press
Life in Victorian Leicester, Jack Simmons, Leics. Museums
Kirby Muxloe Castle, Sir Charles Peers, English Heritage
A Family Guide to Charnwood Forest, Joan Stevenson, Sycamore Press
Domesday Book in Rutland, Prince Yuri Galitzine, Rutland Record Society
The Viking Way, John Stead, Cicerone Press
Bradgate Park, Joan Stevenson and Anthony Squires, Kairos Press
Foxton Locks to Rutland Water, Heather MacDermid, Cordee
For newcomers to walking *Teach Yourself 'Walking and Rambling',* by Heather MacDermid, Hodder and Stoughton, is packed full of interest and information. and for adults new to the joys of walking: *The Gentle Art of Country Walking,* John Wyatt, Century
The Leicestershire County Council publications for children *'The Changing Canals', 'The Passing Trains', 'Water for People'* and *'Belgrave, an 18th C. village'* are well illustrated and informative primary age booklets. County Hall.

Fenny Spring Windmill (Route 8)

95

THE FAMILY WALKS SERIES

The publishers welcome suggestions for future titles and will be pleased to consider manuscripts relating to Derbyshire from new and established authors.

Scarthin Books of Cromford, in the Peak District, are also leading new, second-hand and antiquarian booksellers, and are eager to purchase specialised material, both ancient and modern. Contact Dr. D.J. Mitchell 01629 823272.

JESUS' WOMEN

Thank God for them!

JOY TETLEY

kevin
mayhew

kevin mayhew

First published in Great Britain in 2016 by Kevin Mayhew Ltd
Buxhall, Stowmarket, Suffolk IP14 3BW
Tel: +44 (0) 1449 737978 Fax: +44 (0) 1449 737834
E-mail: info@kevinmayhew.com

www.kevinmayhew.com

9 8 7 6 5 4 3 2 1 0

ISBN 978 1 84867 864 4
Catalogue No. 1501533

Cover design by Rob Mortonson
© Image used under licence from Shutterstock Inc.
Edited by Nicki Copeland
Typeset by Angela Selfe

Printed and bound in Great Britain

Contents

About the author

The Venerable Dr Joy Tetley

Formerly Archdeacon of Worcester, Joy is now focusing on a ministry of prayer, writing, teaching and counsel. She has served in ordained ministry for many years, being involved during this time in parish and cathedral ministry and various forms of theological education. She also has a keen interest in ecumenism and has been involved in a number of ecumenical dialogues. She has a special passion for the Bible and its relevance for today and has produced a number of publications in this area.

Joy Tetley has contributed to the following compilation books for Kevin Mayhew: *Faith Matters* (1501369); *Facing the Issues* (1501353); *More Sermons on Difficult Subjects* (1501389) and written *God Speaking* (1501477).

Introduction

There were, so to speak, a good many women in Jesus' life. The biblical record tells us of the women in his family and family background, the women who befriended and supported him, the women whom he encountered along the way, and the women he included in his teaching. They are a fascinating collection of females and they repay careful attention. Each has her own tale to tell. Each is her own person, important in her own right and in her own time. And all still have something to say to succeeding generations, down to the women and men of our own day.

It is with these women that we shall be engaging in this book. We shall hope to meet them in such a way that they foster (and perhaps provoke) not only our thoughts but also our prayers. We shall approach them, therefore, through what might be described as informed reflections rather than formal studies. These reflections are the preliminary musings of one who, over many years of New Testament study and teaching, has been persistently intrigued and affected by its female characters. They are 'preliminary' in the sense that they are but glimpses, intended to present readers with the stimulus and opportunity to make their own acquaintance with these women and to pursue that relationship in any way that seems helpful.

To facilitate that further, it will be important for readers to look for themselves at the primary biblical material indicated for each character (perhaps reading it out loud, which can often evoke fresh perspectives). As we shall see, the Gospel writers (Matthew, Mark, Luke and John) have varying approaches when presenting us with Jesus' women, relating to their particular understandings of Jesus and his significance. Being aware of this can enrich and clarify the sight (and sound) of the women that we can catch from their writings. It may also help to switch on our own faith imagination, as we seek to meet these women on our own ground.

The reflections can be used in any way which seems appropriate – by individuals, certainly, but they might also fit well into a group scenario. Discussing responses and reactions together can broaden and deepen understanding and enable prayer.

However it is used, may this book put the spotlight on some remarkable women. Thank God for them.

CHAPTER 1

Family (Part 1)

A. Forebears – Matthew's genealogy of Jesus

Overview: what's in a name?

Nowadays, many people are fascinated by their ancestry and there is much research into family trees. We want to know where we have come from in order to understand more fully who we are. Perhaps this interest is fuelled by the kind of culture in which we now live, at least in the West. Strongly individualistic in character, it is marked by the dissolution of old certainties, the reconfiguring of traditional family and community structures, and the rapid, sometimes bewildering emergence of new scientific and technological developments. What does it mean to be human in all this? Where – and to what – do we belong? Do we matter? Such fundamental questions of meaning, even if not consciously articulated, often underlie our delving into lineage, our exploration of the blood line which has been so influential in putting us together.

In the cultural context of the New Testament, family trees – genealogies – also had a prominent place. The reason for this, however, was not grounded in an individual's recreational interest in discovering their past. Life then and there was rather more corporate and community-focused. That being the case, it was important to be able to establish genealogical credentials, both with regard to membership of the people of God as a whole and of a family grouping or tribe in particular. It meant you belonged, and belonging in this way was pretty near the heart of the meaning of your existence. To be an 'outsider' or a 'loner' pushed you to a very undesirable edge.

For two of the New Testament Gospel writers, Matthew and Luke, it was clearly important to set out what they believed to be the human family tree of Jesus. They wanted to demonstrate that Jesus was the culmination of God's purposes for the people of God, not to mention God's purposes for the whole of humankind. Luke underlines this by tracing the genealogy of Jesus back to Adam, the primal human being. Matthew does so by including in Jesus' family line people who did not belong to the chosen people of God. This is rendered more striking by the fact that these outsiders are also women. Both Evangelists wanted to show that God had, so to speak, 'written' the genealogy of Jesus, drawing together all the threads of lineage to make ready for Jesus' birth. In the most significant and essential sense, Jesus 'belonged' in God's plan of salvation for the whole world.

Though the other two Evangelists (Mark and John) undoubtedly shared this conviction, they had a different way of showing it. In Mark's Gospel, Jesus appears apparently out of nowhere but the title of the book gives the key to his origins: 'The beginning of the good news of Jesus Christ, the Son of God' (Mark 1:1). Jesus is *God's* Son. That is the heart of the matter, whatever might be said of his human family tree. John makes the same claim, at greater length and in profoundly theological language (John 1:1-18). From the very beginning of all things, God's only Son has been one with God. And that only Son was made flesh in Jesus. In Jesus, therefore, we can see, if we will, the strange glory of God his Father.

But, humanly speaking, where are the women in Jesus' background? There must, of course, have been many, but, as has been traditional in most cultures, genealogies then were traced through the male line. In the two Gospel genealogies, however, amidst all the fathers, four mothers are also mentioned (five, if Jesus' immediate mother, Mary, be included), and they are all to be found in Matthew's version (Matthew 1:1-17). That in itself is worthy of note because it is not, perhaps, what we might expect. Overall it is Luke, rather than Matthew, who presents us with a fuller and more positive picture of the role of women in the life and ministry of Jesus. That is strikingly illustrated by the role of Mary, the mother of Jesus. As we shall see, her contribution in Luke is decidedly high profile. In Matthew, however, although she has a vital part to play, Mary is given no voice of her own. She is spoken about rather than speaking for herself.

Yet it is Matthew who highlights four other women in Jesus' family line. Looking at who they were may perhaps help us to understand better why this is so. They are all to be found in verses 3-6 of Matthew's opening chapter and, as such, they are embedded in the first of the three sections which make up the genealogy of Jesus according to Matthew. They are thus an integral part of that foundational development of God's people which began with Abraham, the first patriarch, and reached a crucial turning point with David, the second and greatest of Israel's kings. It was from David's line that the longed-for Messiah, the saviour of God's people, was expected to come. After the many trials, tribulations and failures they had been through, God's people believed that God would send a new David, and righteousness and peace would at last have their day.

For Matthew, that Messiah was Jesus, whom he perceived as not only the saviour of God's focal chosen people, the Jews, but also the fulfilment of the vision that is set out most clearly in the prophecy of Isaiah, of the promised one as 'a light to the nations' (Isaiah 49:6). The women he mentions point strongly to that. Tamar (1:3) was a Canaanite, as was Rahab (1:5). Ruth (1:5) was from Moab. Bathsheba (1:6, but not named by Matthew) was 'the wife of Uriah' the Hittite and very possibly of that lineage herself. These women are thus 'outsiders', bringing in new blood, enriching God's people by their presence and their progeny, enabling the working out of God's promise to Abraham that through his descendants all the families of the earth would be blessed.

As we shall see, these women are also, in their various ways, unconventional. Tamar showed great courage and initiative in countering personal and sexual oppression, thereby putting her own life on the line. Rahab was a prostitute who risked everything to effect the rescue of Israelite infiltrators from her Canaanite city. Ruth, the childless widow, severed her roots in her own country to go with her mother-in-law to a new land. There she showed a faithful boldness, which reaped its reward! The wife of Uriah was sexually abused and exploited by the most powerful man in the land, who disposed of her husband in the process. She was, in modern terminology, a 'survivor'. Yet, though she had no formal redress, she was clearly a woman of determination and spirit, as is evidenced by the way she stood up for her son's right of succession. That son duly became the fabled King Solomon.

The women in Matthew's genealogy of Jesus are thus highly significant, in terms of both their background and their experience. They matter. And they point clearly to the mission and character of the one to whose eventual emergence they contributed – to Jesus. Jesus was a boundary-crosser, in terms of both his physical journeying (including Samaritan and Gentile territory) and of his ministry and teaching. He delighted, it seems, in reaching out to those considered by the established cultural code as undesirable or unacceptable, and his teaching constantly challenged rigidly held attitudes. He, too, like the women in his family tree, risked everything for his convictions. And, in his case, he died for his pains – despised, rejected and abused.

Jesus was also unconventional in the way he regarded and related to women. As we shall explore later in this book, again and again he disregarded the cultural norms of his time, and treated women with unaccustomed and public respect – including those of low reputation. He talked publicly with them. That in itself broke convention. Further, he did not talk down to them. He even talked theology with them – and that included with a Samaritan woman 'living in sin' (as it was then considered). One has the distinct impression that Jesus would have warmed to Tamar, Rahab, Ruth and 'the wife of Uriah'!

Indeed, although they belonged to a decidedly patriarchal system, these women were also regarded as 'heroines' in ancient Jewish tradition. Along with other strong and influential women like Deborah, Esther and Judith, they took their place in the cherished story of God's people. Tamar and Bathsheba, in fact, had already been included in important Old Testament genealogies in 1 Chronicles 2 and 3. Tamar is also specifically mentioned at the end of the Book of Ruth, in a prayer of blessing (Ruth 4:12). We should, therefore, duly note that within the tradition expressed in Scripture, there is most certainly a place for the belief that the divine purpose can be worked out through women as well as men.

So now let us look a little more closely at each of Matthew's four founding mothers.

Tamar

Tamar's story can be found in Genesis 38. In many ways it is a shocking narrative, but it is very clear who is the heroine. Tamar is treated appallingly, but she herself seeks to counter this by adopting a bold and very dangerous strategy. She is clearly not a lady to lie down under ill-treatment. So she decides to 'lie down' in a different way in order to shame her father-in-law into giving her justice.

That father-in-law is Judah, one of the most significant of the sons of Jacob and therefore one of the founding fathers of the 12 tribes of Israel. It was from the tribe of Judah that the Davidic dynasty emerged, and from the tribe of Judah that the Messiah was expected to come. And yet, in the episode we are considering, like so many of the leading figures in the early history of Israel, Judah is very much a man behaving badly. As ever, God was kept busy working *all* things together for good, even those things which clearly left much to be desired.

Judah chooses Tamar as a wife for his firstborn son, Er. For a reason which is not specified, Er comes to a sticky end, his death being attributed to God's displeasure. This leaves Tamar as a childless widow. Judah then orders his second son, Onan, to take Tamar to wife, thus fulfilling the then tradition that, in these circumstances, a brother-in-law should 'raise up offspring' for his brother. It appears that Onan is not exactly happy with this arrangement. He obeys his father up to a point – in this case, the crucial one. He 'spilled his semen on the ground', we are told (Genesis 38:9). His partial obedience does not save him. 'Spilt seed' is regarded as a serious offence against the Creator, and Onan pays for it with his life.

Judah has one more son, Shelah. It should now be the case that he fulfils the duty of a brother-in-law in relation to Tamar.

Indeed, Judah promises Tamar that this will be the situation when Shelah is of age. So she agrees to remain a widow in her father's house until a marriage can take place. She has put up with a fair amount already and is now prepared to take on this further trial. But it eventually becomes apparent to her that, though Shelah has now grown up, Judah's promise is not going to be delivered. No doubt he fears his one remaining son might suffer the same fate as the other two.

Not surprisingly, Tamar has had enough. She hatches a clever, if decidedly risky, plan and delivers it in a very canny way. She pretends to be a prostitute and, with veiled face, lures Judah into her clutches. But not before she has demanded a pledge from him in advance of her fee (this latter being 'a kid from the flock'). The pledge is, in fact, rather more valuable than the kid. What she demands and receives is Judah's signet and cord, and the staff that is in his hand – clear means of identification. When Judah sends his friend (note) to duly make his payment and claim back his pledge, no sign of the 'prostitute' can be found, and no one in the area is aware of her existence. Not wanting to become a laughing stock, he decides to let the matter drop and relinquish his pledge.

Tamar, however, has other ideas. As a result of this liaison with her father-in-law, she has become pregnant. When her pregnancy becomes evident, Judah roundly condemns her and orders that she be burned to death. Like stoning, this was one of the awful penalties that was then in place for the offence of 'playing the whore'. Judah is soon to learn, however, that in Tamar's case, 'playing the whore' has a somewhat different meaning. She has 'staged' the whole episode and 'performed' this role specifically to expose his shortcomings. On the verge of being executed, she produces the pledged articles, saying, 'It was the owner of these who made me pregnant.' Judah can hardly deny that they are his, but to his credit, he does at least have the grace to acknowledge his transgression (though we may feel that it is a less than absolute repentance). He declares, 'She is more in the right than I, since I did not give her my son, Shelah.'

So Tamar is saved from her fate. She gives birth to twins, Perez and Zerah. Through Perez she contributes to that line which ultimately produces King David and, in official genealogical terms at least, that longed-for Saviour, 'born of David's line' – Jesus.

Thankfully (and interestingly) her role in this regard is not suppressed, as we might have expected, but openly affirmed in the tradition. She has left her mark.

Rahab *(Joshua 2:1-21; 6:17, 22-25)*

We move from a woman who was 'playing the whore' to one whose actual profession it was. Rahab is a prostitute in Jericho at the time when the Israelites, after their exodus from Egypt and many years of wandering in the wilderness, are poised to take the land of Canaan. They are particularly eyeing up Jericho. As part of their reconnaissance, two spies are sent into the city. These infiltrators find their way to Rahab's house and spend the night there. They are not the only 'spies' around, however, and their visit is reported to the king of Jericho, who promptly sends orders to Rahab to deliver up her clients.

This leaves Rahab with a dilemma. The easiest and safest course of action would be to comply with the king's command. But Rahab has a canny eye to the future. She is well aware of the Israelite threat to her city, not to mention the land as a whole. And she has heard something of the backstory of this invading people (Joshua 2:9-11). She is in awe of their God and is convinced that the city will fall to them. As she puts it to the men she is hiding, 'I know that the Lord has given you the land, and that dread of you has fallen on us, and that all the inhabitants of the land melt in fear before you' (Joshua 2:9).

But not Rahab. She does not do 'melting in fear', it seems. Rather, she sees in her present predicament an opportunity to ensure the future safety of herself and her family. She therefore takes the risk of deceiving the king and putting him off the scent. She claims she did not know who her visitors were, and that in any case they have already left the city. She then bargains with the spies whom she has hidden under flax on her roof. 'Now then,' she says, 'since I have dealt kindly with you, swear to me by the Lord that you in turn will deal kindly with my family. Give me a sign of good faith that you will spare my father and mother, my brothers and sisters, and all who belong to them, and deliver our lives from death' (Joshua 2:12, 13).

They come to an agreement: provided she does not 'talk', and she ties a crimson cord in her window, she and her family will be spared, come the conquest of the city. She then lets the men down by a rope from her window, her house being conveniently situated on the outer side of the city wall (Joshua 2:15-21).

When the time comes, the agreement is duly honoured (Joshua 6:17, 22-25) and, as the biblical writer puts it, 'her family has lived in Israel ever since' (6:25). And according to Matthew the Evangelist (whose genealogy, it has to be said, is based more on a theological schema than on strict chronology), Rahab contributes to the official family line of Jesus by becoming the mother of Boaz and therefore the great-great-grandmother of King David (Matthew 1:5, 6).

What a strong and resourceful woman to have in one's lineage.

No wonder the author of the letter to the Hebrews included her in his great catalogue of exemplars of faith (Hebrews 11:31). She remains an example to us.

Ruth

Ruth's story is one of the most affecting and attractive narratives in the whole of Scripture. It is a story of love and faithfulness. And it has the added bonus of a happy ending. Ruth gets her man!

But, of course, it is not only a romantic tale well told. It highlights an important aspect of King David's lineage – that his bloodline includes a foreign woman, and one, moreover, whose qualities are more than consonant with the values of God's people Israel. Not for the first or the last time, God is working out the divine purpose through an outsider.

Ruth the foreigner comes from Moab, a land to the east of the Dead Sea. She becomes involved with Israel's story through an Israelite family who moved to Moab to find food, at a time of famine in their homeland. As the writer tells us (Ruth 1:1), this was 'in the days when the judges ruled' in Israel – not the most stable period in its history. No doubt Elimelech and his wife Naomi thought Moab would provide both sustenance and security for themselves and their two sons, Mahlon and Chilion. They came from Bethlehem (which, ironically in their circumstances, means 'house of bread'), and Moab was not too far distant.

Relations between Moab and Israel had not always been good, however. And the ill-feeling had by no means been consigned to history, as a stark passage from Deuteronomy indicates:

> No Ammonite or Moabite shall be admitted to the assembly of the Lord. Even to the tenth generation, none of their

descendants shall be admitted to the assembly of the Lord, because they did not meet you with food and water on your journey out of Egypt, and because they hired against you Balaam son of Beor . . . to curse you . . . You shall never promote their welfare or their prosperity as long as you live.

Deuteronomy 23:3-6

But the book of Ruth shows nothing of this attitude. Indeed, the situation is reversed, not to say redeemed. Now Moab provides needy Israelites with food, and a Moabite woman brings Israel blessing.

But this positive tale is not without its tragic dimension. While in Moab, Elimelech dies. Mahlon and Chilion both take Moabite wives – Orpah and Ruth – but after some years, they, too, both die. As the writer puts it, 'the woman was left without her two sons or her husband' (Ruth 1:5). What this means to Naomi is aptly summed up in her words to her compatriots when she returns to Bethlehem:

'Call me no longer Naomi [meaning 'pleasant'],
call me Mara [meaning 'bitter'],
for the Almighty has dealt bitterly with me.
I went away full,
but the Lord has brought me back empty;
why call me Naomi when the Lord has dealt harshly
    with me,
and the Almighty has brought calamity upon me?'

Ruth 1:20, 21

Clearly, and not surprisingly, Naomi is a very unhappy lady. But, in fact, she has not returned 'empty'. With her is her Moabite daughter-in-law, Ruth. The episode where Orpah eventually takes her leave of Naomi while Ruth insists on going with her is beautifully and movingly described (Ruth 1:6-18). Ruth's character shines through in her response to Naomi, when her mother-in-law tries to persuade her to turn back and find her future in her own land.

> 'Do not press me to leave you
> or to turn back from following you!
> Where you go, I will go;
> where you lodge, I will lodge;
> your people shall be my people,
> and your God my God.
> Where you die, I will die –
> there will I be buried.
> May the Lord do thus and so to me,
> and more as well,
> if even death parts me from you.'
>
> *Ruth 1:16, 17*

This is a bereaved young widow speaking, one who surely also has cause to be bitter. Yet there is no trace of that in her behaviour or her words. Love, commitment and courage are her dominant traits. She will stay with Naomi through thick and thin, even though that means being bereaved of her homeland as well as her husband.

These character traits remain much in evidence as she first gleans for Naomi and then (with Naomi's connivance) 'harvests' a new husband in Boaz, who turns out to be the family's near kinsman. The way she does this is almost brazen. The writer tells us that one night she visits the threshing floor and lies down at the feet of Boaz. It is perhaps not without relevance that 'feet' was a common euphemism for a somewhat more sensitive area. No wonder Boaz is startled when he wakes up!

Happily, Boaz does the right thing and follows the required procedure (Ruth 3–4). He then marries Ruth and a son is born to them. Ruth's life is transformed, and Naomi can once again enter into the meaning of her name. Life becomes more than 'pleasant' for her. And the child Obed in due course becomes the father of Jesse, who becomes the father of David.

In both a personal and a dynastic sense, Ruth's story has proved fruitful indeed – another case of God working all things together for good.

The wife of Uriah (2 Samuel 11:1–12:24)

In Matthew's genealogy, Bathsheba, very pointedly, is not referred to by her name. Though by the time of Solomon's birth she is married to King David, she is still described as 'the wife of Uriah' (Matthew 1:6). The way in which she becomes David's wife does this great Israelite king no credit whatsoever. His behaviour is shameful. At least that is fully acknowledged in the Scriptural record – and very emphatically so by the prophet Nathan, who tells David an acutely apposite little parable to drive his message home. Nathan's 'punchline' – *You are the man* – clearly reaches its target (2 Samuel 12:1-15). There is no attempt at a cover-up. David's sin is laid bare, both at the time and in the tradition.

Having seen the naked Bathsheba bathing, the king gives way to his lust, taking advantage of her and grossly abusing his power. She is currently the wife of Uriah the Hittite, a soldier away from home fighting the king's battles. Bathsheba is a victim/survivor of sexual abuse, perpetrated by one who has complete authority over her. And his treatment of her results in pregnancy.

The matter gets even worse. David compounds his wrongdoing by trying to get Uriah to sleep with Bathsheba, so that he will then assume he is the father of the child and leave David in the clear. He brings Uriah back from the front, but in spite of every strategy he adopts (including getting Uriah drunk) he cannot persuade him to lie with his wife. Unlike his king at this point, Uriah has some integrity. His comrades are camping in the field, observing the disciplines of battle-readiness. He will not break ranks and treat himself to home comforts of any sort. As he puts it to David, 'I will not do such a thing' (2 Samuel 11:6-13). David then sends him back to the front, carrying a letter to his commander which, unbeknown to its carrier, contains instructions to ensure that Uriah is so positioned in battle that he is killed in action. Those instructions are duly carried out.

So Bathsheba is abused and then widowed by the sin (there is no other word for it) of a king who is the Lord's anointed. He does at least then take her as one of his wives. Their first child, conceived by his abuse, dies, that being interpreted as God's judgement on David's sin (2 Samuel 12:14-23). Their second child is Solomon, who in due course becomes one of Israel's most fabled monarchs (though he, too, is not without his failings).

How Bathsheba felt about what happened to her is not revealed to us. Unlike Tamar, Rahab and Ruth, she is not given a voice. She is the silent recipient of unpleasant circumstances she did not ask for (like so many down the ages). But we do hear something from her many years later, towards the end of David's life. And what we hear suggests that she is a woman of some strength and determination. She faces the king with his promise that Solomon would succeed him on the throne, a promise which is threatened by the usurpation of another of

David's sons (by another wife). After all she has been through, she is more than prepared to stand up for her son's rights (1 Kings 1:11-31). But what she makes of her own treatment remains untold. We can only imagine.

B. Mary, the mother of Jesus

Overview: Mary according to the four Gospel writers

Our Lady, as she is often known, was clearly quite a lady! For 2000 years Mary has meant many things to many people. She is not exactly 'Mary, Mary quite contrary', but she has excited a great deal of attention and not a few sharply contrary assessments. Devotion and controversy have both accrued to her, in significant measure. Theologians have poured many words over her. Greater and lesser artists and poets, in many and various ways, have sought to present her to us. She has been caught up in church politics – not least the kind that have involved torture and bloodshed. She has been 'claimed' by this group and that for their own purposes. But through it all, as with her son and Lord, Mary's own truth and holiness shine through. So what are we to make of her?

In terms of her specific vocation, Mary's role was, without doubt, unique. She brought Jesus into this world. Thank God for her, therefore. Yet in a very real and more general sense, her calling is that of all those committed to Jesus: to receive and to minister God's saving grace; to be the bearer of the good news of Jesus Christ. As well as celebrating her particular contribution, then, we can and should look to her as *an icon of Christian discipleship* – a way in to discerning more clearly how *we* might bring Jesus into the world.

It is worth asking ourselves what we see in Mary and what we can learn from her. The answer might be more than we perhaps expect.

There is no better place to start looking than the New Testament. Indeed, looking at Mary through the eyes of the four Evangelists is a fascinating and challenging thing to do. As they do with Jesus, Matthew, Mark, Luke and John each present us with a different perspective, a distinctive portrait of Mary. They are manifestly giving us a glimpse of the same woman, but in each case varying characteristics come to the fore, thus giving us a fuller picture of who she was, and supplying a range of encouraging indicators for those who would also be 'servants of the Lord'.

When looking at these four pen-portraits, Luke's is the obvious one with which to start. According to tradition, Luke was a painter as well as a doctor. He certainly excels in verbal artistry, not least in relation to Mary. Over the centuries, his presentation of her has not only attracted theological debate; it has also inspired painters, poets and musicians innumerable to produce some of their finest work. Creativity continues to sparkle from Luke's telling out of the creativity of God.

Mary features prominently in the early chapters of Luke's Gospel narrative. She is there also at the beginning of his second volume, the Acts of the Apostles. There, after the Ascension, the followers of Jesus are gathered in prayer, awaiting the promised 'power from on high' (Luke 24:49). It is interesting that in both cases, Mary is directly associated with the overshadowing, the in-breaking of the Holy Spirit. In the first instance, this is a hidden mystery; in the second, it is dramatic and highly public. Either way, Mary is open to the creative operation of God's Spirit, whether during her encounter with the angel Gabriel or at Pentecost; whether issuing in the birth of the Son of God or the birth of his Church. But she is no mere passive recipient. She is evidently given to *questing and questioning, pondering and praying.*

At the Annunciation, even with an angel in front of her, Mary tries to work out what is going on ('she was much perplexed by his words and pondered what sort of greeting this might be', Luke 1:29), and she is not afraid to ask a very direct and pertinent question of her supernatural visitor: 'How can this be, since I am a virgin?' (Luke 1:34). Good question. As, indeed, is her question of the 12-year-old Jesus, found at last in the Temple: 'Why have you treated us like this?' (Luke 2:48).

'How can this be . . . ?' 'Why have you treated us like this?' These are also valid questions of discipleship. We recognise them, and Mary shows us how to utter them, boldly and confidently, in the very presence of God – even as she also shows us how important it is to treasure and ponder profound experiences we do not fully understand: 'Mary treasured all these words and pondered them in her heart' (Luke 2:19).

Luke's Mary is *direct, prayerful, thoughtful – and positive.* Once she has expressed her questioning to the angel, she accepts her mission with a very definite 'amen': 'Let it be with me according to your word' (Luke 1:38). *Fiat,* as the Latin translation has it. Let it happen. This is no passive submission. This is an unequivocal 'yes' to sharing in God's work of new creation – whatever the cost.

We then realise that Luke's Mary is also 'Magnificat woman' – singing a song of exultation that God has invited *her,* she of low estate, to share in God's great enterprise – that of bringing into the world the radical values of the kingdom of heaven (Luke 1:46-55).

John's Mary is not a million miles removed from Luke's portrait. Though never given her proper name (she is always 'the mother of Jesus'), she is characterised as *feisty and faithful, provocative and persistent.* Again, her role is associated with beginnings and endings (which, in truth, turn out to be new beginnings). She provokes Jesus (there is no other word for it – Jesus is clearly irritated by her behaviour) into performing the first of his signs at Cana in Galilee. She will not take no for an answer – and water is turned into wine, signalling the new and best wine of God's kingdom (John 2:1-11).

The mother of Jesus is also there at the climactic sign of Golgotha, supporting her own flesh and blood as he is cruelly destroyed (John 19:25-27). Here she quite literally faces up to the loss of all she had hoped for, believed in and loved. How is that for courageous and determined discipleship? And just as blood and water attended his birth, so the blood and water that issue at his death (John 19:34) signify new birth, new creation, new life and hope. The part of his mother in all this is crucial.

When we turn to Mark, we are given yet another perspective on Mary. There is no reference in this Gospel to the birth and childhood of Jesus, but his mother appears on the scene early on in his public ministry (Mark 3:21, 31-34). With other family members, she tries to extract him from the encircling crowds and increasingly dangerous publicity. She fears, as we might put it these days, that he has 'lost it', and is anxious to protect him, not least from himself. The rebuke she receives from Jesus makes it very clear to her that this is an interference too far.

And Matthew's perspective? Here Mary has a vital role in the fulfilment of God's promise of salvation – but she has no voice. Others speak about her and on her behalf – but she is not afforded the opportunity to speak for herself – like so many voiceless and vulnerable ones down the ages. Yet a world-changing and dangerous mission is being asked of her – dangerous to both her reputation and her life. She could have been stoned to death for bringing shame on herself and her family. It is fortunate that Joseph is 'a righteous man' (Matthew 1:19), because he clearly doesn't believe Mary's story. Divine intervention is needed to convince him, and thus ensure that Mary survives and Emmanuel becomes a reality. Never has silence become more eloquent. One who is hidden and disgraced becomes the agent of God's overwhelming and saving grace. God does, indeed, move in mysterious ways. We should never underestimate the voiceless, and what God might be saying and doing through them.

Quite a lady, then, this Mary – whichever way we look at her. In pondering her more carefully, especially through the portraits of the Evangelists, we may find deep resonance and encouragement for our own vocation and ministry, whatever that might be. For we, too, whatever our gender, have our part to play in bringing Jesus into the world.

So let us look at each of those Gospel portraits a little more closely.

Luke's portrait of Mary

The Annunciation

Luke introduces us to Mary in the opening section of his Gospel, where she is the key figure in that dramatic event known as the Annunciation (Luke 1:26-38). The event is perhaps familiar to us from many a nativity play and carol service, where its meaning and impact can be diluted in an ocean of sentiment. But Luke has something more profound (and more challenging) in mind. The angel Gabriel (an archangel no less) is sent by God to a young woman in Nazareth of Galilee. We are to note straightaway that she is from an ordinary town, located (as we might put it) out in the provinces. She is not from the big and holy city of Jerusalem, that centre of the religious and political establishment. Indeed, Galilee tended to be looked down upon by those within Jerusalem's respectable confines. It was regarded as far too lax in its religious observances, and it housed folk from all over the place. 'Galilee of the Gentiles' was its nickname. It is to this region that God sends Gabriel, with a momentous message. Not for the first time, God is about to work out the divine purpose in a surprising way.

The young woman chosen for this world-changing operation of the Holy Spirit is called Mary, and she is betrothed (engaged/promised) to a man called Joseph. In all probability she is in her early teens. At that time and in that culture, girls were often betrothed to their future husbands from the age of 13. Though marriage and therefore marital relations came later, strict faithfulness was expected from the point of betrothal, with severe consequences for those who went astray. A young woman who fell pregnant, and not by her betrothed, risked certain shame and possible death (stoning was the legal penalty). It is in Matthew's Gospel where this aspect of Mary's situation is highlighted, but awareness of it perhaps helps to inform our understanding of her responses as set out in Luke's account. This young girl has some courage to say 'yes'.

Mary's betrothed, Joseph, is 'of the house of David' (Luke 1:27), but we are not told anything further about Mary's background. Joseph's lineage is sufficient to establish the legal connection between Mary's son and David's line – that line from which it was expected that the longed-for Messiah would come, the one who would save God's people. But, humanly speaking, it is from Mary that the Messiah will be born, fruit of Mary's 'yes' and God's creative activity. Joseph (generously) provides the legal credentials and personal support.

For Luke, Mary is the main human focus of this episode. For him, it is important to stress Mary's status as a virgin, so that we are left in no doubt that God's great work of salvation in Jesus is directly the work of God. But she is not just any virgin. She is given a name, albeit a common one at the time, and that plus her behaviour make her a particular individual with a unique contribution to make. It is *Mary* who makes possible the coming of God in flesh. She could have refused.

But she does not. Nonetheless, her acceptance is not immediate or unquestioning. Mary is clearly someone who ponders on things, who tries to work things out, who wants to make some sense of what is happening.

Her encounter with the angel Gabriel is, to put it mildly, a startling experience. Yet she is not so overcome by it that her thought processes are overwhelmed. Rather than fainting on the spot at Gabriel's appearance, she is 'much perplexed by his words and pondered what sort of greeting this might be' (Luke 1:29).

She immediately begins to engage with this strange eruption into her life. So when Gabriel delivers his momentous message, she straightaway cottons on to its implications. And she is not so afraid that she cannot come out directly with the obvious question that has sprung into her mind: 'How can this be, since I am a virgin?' (Luke 1:34).

Even in the midst of a traumatic spiritual experience, Mary can *question* both God's messenger and God's message.

Significantly, as in the case of other great biblical questioners such as Job, this is not held against her. Quite the reverse. It draws out from Gabriel what is the very heart of the matter: 'The Holy Spirit will come upon you, and the power of the Most High will overshadow you; therefore the child to be born will be holy; he will be called Son of God' (Luke 1:35).

The implications of Mary's response for our discipleship are clear. It is right that we try to make sense of things. It is right that when we do not understand – particularly at times of trauma or crisis – we should bring our questions directly and unambiguously to God.

Gabriel's response emboldens Mary to express her critical acceptance of God's will. 'Then Mary said, "Here am I, the servant of the Lord; let it be with me according to your word"' (Luke 1:38). As we have seen, this is not an unquestioning, passive act of compliance. Mary is not a 'yes woman' in this sense. This is not a fatalistic 'whatever you say', nor a craven attempt to curry favour: as Gabriel has made clear, Mary has already found favour with God.

Mary's 'yes', born of honest engagement, is something far more positive. It is an identifying with that divine, creative 'yes', whereby God brings all things to birth. *Fiat* is the word used of God's speech in the Latin translation of Genesis 1's creation narrative. '*Fiat*', says God at the beginning of all things: 'Let it be.'

'*Fiat mihi* . . .' says Mary at the Annunciation. 'Let it be with me according to your word.'

As the Holy Spirit brooded over the primal darkness that it might bring forth light and life, so, as a result of Mary's 'yes', that same Spirit overshadowed the darkness of her womb that she might bring forth the Son of God.

This is awesome. Such a crucial, creative moment is not to be repeated. And yet there are powerful indicators here for our discipleship. Mary's 'yes prayer' should be the prayer of the whole Church, and of each one of us. So we might, for example, ask ourselves questions such as these:

- In what ways do *we* say 'yes' to God?
- *Do* we, indeed, say 'yes' to God?
- And if we do, is it a labour of love? Is it a creative cry, even if it has to be in the midst of pain and anguish?
- How are *we* God's 'yes people'?

Julian of Norwich, back in fourteenth-century England, perhaps had some sage advice for us in this regard. During her revelatory near-death experience, this young woman had a vision of Mary, which she described like this:

> In my spirit, I saw her as though she were physically present, a simple, humble girl, still in her youth, and little more than a child. God showed me something of her spiritual wisdom and honesty, and I understood her profound reverence when she saw her God and Maker; how reverently she marvelled that he should be born of his own creature, and of one so simple. This wisdom and honesty . . . moved her to say to Gabriel in her utter humility, 'Behold the handmaid of the Lord!'
>
> Julian of Norwich, *Revelations of Divine Love*, chapter 4[1]

As so often, Julian sees into the heart of the matter. Wisdom, honesty, humility. Profound reverence and intuitive insight. And this from one who was 'little more than a child'. These are the qualities we all need, whatever age we might be, if we too are to recognise God's often surprising visitations

---

1. Penguin Classics, 1988 reprint edition, p.67.

and respond to God's often unexpected call. They are the qualities the Church needs if it is to bring Jesus into the midst of the changes and chances of this fleeting but (all too often) hurting and hurtful world. But, in our human frailty, we can only have a hope of bearing such qualities if we consent to the overshadowing of God's Spirit in our own lives and contexts. Mary powerfully reminds us that we should ever be open to the presence of God, in whatever way that manifests itself.

The Visitation (Luke 1:39-56)

As well as the main substance of his message, Gabriel gives Mary some interesting additional information. Her kinswoman Elizabeth is also pregnant. 'In her old age,' says Gabriel, Elizabeth 'has also conceived a son; and this is the sixth month for her who was said to be barren.' Then comes Gabriel's 'punchline', which says it all – not only in relation to Elizabeth but also in regard to God's dealings with Mary. Indeed, it is an emphatic summary statement of the whole character of God. 'For nothing will be impossible with God' (Luke 1:36, 37).

Luke tells us that, having heard all this, 'Mary set out and went with haste to a Judean town in the hill country, where she entered the house of Zechariah and greeted Elizabeth' (Luke 1:39, 40). We shall look a little later at Elizabeth in her own right, but for now we focus on that meeting between the two women, known to the Church as the Visitation.

It is a momentous meeting. Yet at the same time, it is so ordinary, so unremarkable. Two expectant mothers coming together to share their feelings, their hopes, dreams and fears. Two women bonded by a common experience, a common joy – understanding and affirming one another, intuitively and in the language of their bodies as well as in their words. Such meetings have happened countless times. And God is concerned with them all – this God who works in and through the ordinary, the everyday.

But this particular womanly meeting has about it more than a touch of the extraordinary. Each woman is hugging a secret slowly taking shape within her. Both expectant mothers are coming to terms with the unexpected. And the destinies of their unborn children are inextricably – painfully – intertwined. These children are to change the world – and break their mothers' hearts.

For now, the dominant feelings are joy, exultation, excitement, anticipation.

For Elizabeth, her pregnancy is hope born out of hopelessness; against all the odds, the longing of her heart fulfilled. For years she has been barren, empty in more senses than one, her personal frustration compounded by the cultural conviction of the time that childlessness meant failure and was a sign of God's disfavour. Now, against all expectations, the impossible has happened. And at first she can hardly believe it. She hides herself away until she is sure. Elizabeth's child is something of a miracle.

Mary's child is even more so. For Mary, pregnancy is something unsought, something, almost literally, out of the blue. As we have seen, when she arose and went with haste into the hill country of Judea to meet her older relative Elizabeth, she had just had her life turned upside down by a visitation from the angel Gabriel. Now she has to bear the consequences of her 'yes' to God. 'Here am I, the servant of the Lord,' she has said; 'let it be with me according to your word.' She feels a great sense of rejoicing – of God's purposes coming to birth in her – even in *her*. But she also knows, surely, that the future will not be easy. She is betrothed, unmarried and pregnant. Even at this time, visiting angels are not an entirely convincing explanation. What must she be thinking and feeling as she hurries along her uphill journey? A whole maelstrom of emotions must be stirring within her.

When Mary arrives and greets her, Elizabeth also feels a stirring, caused by her unborn child leaping in her womb. That child later becomes known as John the Baptist. At this stage, the stirrings of the unborn John bring joy to both women and provoke Mary's exultant song, the Magnificat. Later he brings a different kind of disturbance – a moral and religious challenge to the nation which provokes both conversion and condemnation. His straight-talking honesty lands him in prison, plunging him into a darkness of doubt. And his life is brutally ended by a corrupt, power-hungry weakling of a king. Such a promising beginning brought to such a dreadful end.

Mary's son fares little better. Yet, in the wilderness, Elizabeth's son points to him as the one longed for down the ages, God's promised Saviour, just as Gabriel said. But in the end, the worst happens. Mary's son is condemned to death, fighting out his last hours on one of the most agonising instruments of torture humankind has so far invented. And his mother watches it – watches her son die.

Where is Magnificat now?

Where is God?

All that joy and hope swallowed up in pain, shame, injustice and disgrace.

And yet, as Mary surely will come to see, despite the sword which pierces her soul, the fulfilment of Magnificat is exalted on that bitter cross. Here the mighty have indeed been put down from their thrones, and the lowly, steadfast love of God lifted up. Here, those who acknowledge their emptiness are filled with the goodness of God. Here, the true character of God's strength and mercy is revealed. Here in the cross is the focal icon of God's help, God's kingdom, God's sovereignty, God's salvation. Who would have thought it? What the Lord has spoken to Mary and through her in her song has truly been fulfilled – but in the most surprising, not to say shocking, way.

This proves to be the meaning of the secret that both Elizabeth and Mary – those two ordinary/extraordinary women – are bringing to birth. As yet, the cross has not clouded the horizon, but they know well enough that God is decisively at work – the God whose coming lifts up the lowly and gives their comeuppance to the proud, the God who brings justice and joy. And as it turns out, this is the God who, for his pains, ends up crucified – only to break out again from a womb-like tomb into the fresh air of the Easter garden. 'Established religion' (in whatever guise) has ever found this God difficult, trying to manage this inconvenient deity by containment and careful definition ('the word made flesh made word again', as Edwin Muir has it in his poem, 'The Incarnate One').

But how could joy not well up as Mary and Elizabeth sense the utterly amazing in-breaking and out-breaking of God? It is a secret they must (quite literally) let out – or it cannot achieve its purpose. Let it lead where it will, they will go with it.

The Magnificat has been prayed and sung by many down the ages. It is a staple of the formal liturgy of the Church, particularly at the services of Vespers and Evensong. It has been set to music by any number of composers, but some, arguably, have not quite caught the biblical context of Mary's song (or, perhaps, we should more appropriately call it Mary's outburst!). The content needs to be seen in the light of this context.

The Magnificat did not have its birth from the confines and atmosphere of a religious building. It erupted from the hill country of Judea. Like the overshadowing of the Holy Spirit, it is a breath of fresh air. Indeed, it is reminiscent of another great song of exultation from Israel's heritage – that of Hannah, as recorded in 1 Samuel 2:1-10. Hannah was giving thanks for the gift of her son Samuel, for whose conception and birth she had prayed in great anguish (see 1 Samuel 1). She, like Mary after her, was doing that by singing out her faith in a radical God, the God who brings justice for the oppressed and 'raises up the poor from the dust' (1 Samuel 2:8). Neither Hannah's song nor Mary's Magnificat is a safe and sanitised holy composition. The God they exalt is not a comfortable deity.

For Mary, this moment is euphoric, yet fraught with danger. But this is a young woman of proper confidence and courage. Like her song, she is exultant and edgy, faithful and feisty. She will have to go through much. But how right it is that all generations should call her blessed.

Expectant with the unexpected. So were Mary and Elizabeth. And not only they. Whoever dares to say 'yes' to God will be called to give birth to God's often surprising purposes – and whatever form they take, those purposes will always bear the face of Jesus and the imprint of his wounds. Inherent always, whatever the challenging travail required, will be the joy and alleluia of God. For in the life of God, love and alleluia are inseparable, even when they enter the heart of darkness.

This is a divine secret which must ever come out. We are called to play our part in bringing it to birth. Whatever the cost, we shall never regret it.

CHAPTER 2

Family (Part 2)

Luke's portrait of Mary (contd.)

The Nativity (Luke 2:1-20)

Luke's beautiful narrative describing the birth of Jesus is full of meaning, which familiarity and Christmas tradition can all too easily obscure. It speaks of the breaking of God into the world to bring salvation and peace – something longed for by the people of God down the ages. But when God acts to meet this longing, it is not in the way we might have expected. Even the message of Gabriel to Mary at the Annunciation might have suggested some cataclysmic event. But God's Son, when he comes, is hidden away in a manger, a common animal feeding trough. The only fanfare to celebrate his coming is a jubilant chorus sung by a host of angels. But that is in the night – and the only people who hear it are ordinary shepherds getting on with their job. This is a strange mystery.

What might Mary make of it all? Heavily pregnant ('great with child', as the old AV translation has it), Mary – probably not seated on the proverbial donkey! – trudges with Joseph her betrothed from home in Nazareth to 'the city of David called Bethlehem'. It is a journey of some 85 miles, a challenging journey that in her condition she could surely have done without. The reason for it was a decree of the Roman Emperor (Galilee and Judea were at this time part of the Roman Empire) that there should be a general registration of his people, no doubt for tax purposes. For this process, everyone has to go to their town of origin. In Joseph's case, this is Bethlehem because, as Luke tells us, 'he was descended from the house and family of David' (Luke 2:4).

And when they arrive there, there proves to be no suitable accommodation. Mary's time has come and she has to give birth in an area reserved for animals, placing her newborn in their feeding trough. Such conditions are, to say the least, far from ideal. The most that could be said is that it would be reasonably warm.

To Mary, this must feel some distance from the expectations aroused by Gabriel's words concerning the child who would emerge from her: 'He will be great, and will be called the Son of the Most High, and the Lord God will give to him the throne of his ancestor David. He will reign over the house of Jacob for ever, and of his kingdom there will be no end' (1:32, 33). Yet here she is, labouring in discomfort and obscurity, with only a manger in which to lay her child. It is hardly a kingly context. Perhaps her 'Magnificat' was premature.

And then comes the visitation of the shepherds and their amazing tale of what has happened to them out in the dark fields. They experienced an outbreak of angels! One of these angels calmed their fear with an astounding message: 'Do not be afraid; for see – I am bringing you good news of great joy for all the people: to you is born this day in the city of David a Saviour, who is the Messiah, the Lord.' What is more, he gave them the most surprising sign that the message was true: 'This will be a sign for you: you will find a child wrapped in bands of cloth and lying in a manger' (Luke 2:10-12).

This must have come as a mighty reassurance for Mary – a confirmation that she did indeed hear Gabriel aright. Perhaps, too, it has not escaped this canny woman that her son, though born in such unpromising circumstances, has nonetheless been born in the city of David – 'royal David's city' – a city which, of old, has been prophesied as the birthplace of the coming Messiah (see Micah 5:2). God is surely up to something – and something very significant.

Certainly, according to Luke, Mary responds to the shepherds' visit in a way that is true to her character: 'But Mary treasured all these words and pondered them in her heart' (Luke 2:19). She lets it all sink in, pondering and no doubt puzzling, but knowing in the depths of her spirit that God is doing something profoundly special. Luke's Mary is thus a 'theologian' in the truest sense – prayerfully exploring and probing the workings of God. In the culture of the time, when theology was not considered to be the realm of women, it is worthy of note that Luke presents Mary to us in this way. As we shall see, though Mary is pre-eminent, she is not the only woman whom Luke will show to us in this light.

The Presentation (Luke 2:22-40)

Luke stresses to us that Mary and Joseph, as faithful members of God's people, are careful to observe all that the Jewish Law requires in relation to the birth of a son – particularly a firstborn son. So, eight days after the birth, as is customary, the child is circumcised and named (2:21). Following Gabriel's instructions at the Annunciation, he is called Jesus – a name which means 'God saves'.

The next ritual observance has a dual aspect – the purification of Mary and the presentation of the child to God in the Temple at Jerusalem (the central place of worship for the people of God). It is interesting to note that this dual aspect has led to a dual naming for the feast with which the Christian Church marks this event. Sometimes it is known as the feast of the Purification of the Blessed Virgin Mary; sometimes (more often nowadays) as the Presentation of Christ in the Temple, and sometimes as both. Indeed, both aspects are important in Luke's account. And both point to Mary's faithfulness.

The Law required that a woman should go through a process of ritual purification after the birth of a child. This had to happen 40 days after the birth of a male child and 80 days after the birth of a girl. It was connected to the belief that certain things, like the emission of bodily fluids, rendered a person ritually unclean. So until she had been through this ritual, a woman was not supposed to touch anything sacred or to enter the Temple. The old practice of 'churching' in Christian culture is reminiscent of this.

Mary duly observes this requirement. The offered sacrifice which Luke mentions – 'a pair of turtle-doves or two young pigeons' (Luke 2:24) – completes the purification ritual. As the book of Leviticus puts it, when the days of a woman's purification are completed:

> She shall bring to the priest at the entrance of the tent of meeting a lamb in its first year for a burnt-offering, and a pigeon or a turtle-dove for a sin-offering. He shall offer it before the Lord, and make atonement on her behalf; then she shall be clean from her flow of blood. This is the law for her who bears a child, male or female. If she cannot afford a sheep, she shall take two turtle-doves or two pigeons, one for a burnt-offering and the other for a sin-offering; and the priest shall make atonement on her behalf, and she shall be clean.
>
> *Leviticus 12:6-8*

We notice that Mary clearly comes within the category of those too poor to manage the standard offering. The one whose kingdom will have no end is born of a woman at the lesser end of the social scale. She is, indeed, of 'low estate' (Luke 1:48, RSV). There, as Mary might put it, is something to ponder.

In their visit to Jerusalem, Mary and Joseph also observe the Jewish Law's direction that every firstborn male should be presented to the Lord (see Exodus 13:11-16; 22:29; Nehemiah 10:35, 36). Perhaps, in addition, Mary has a sense of following in Hannah's footsteps. As we have seen in her Magnificat song, Mary has already echoed Hannah's outburst of exultation. Does she now feel a further affinity with this woman from her Jewish heritage? Hannah came to the sacred place at Shiloh and, via the priest, handed over her special son, Samuel, to the Lord, dedicating the child to the Lord's service. Mary, too, is recognising that her special child, with all the mystery of his coming, belongs to God. It is a lesson she will have to relearn – and in a way that will not exactly be comfortable.

For now, there is yet more to take into the treasury of her thoughts and prayers. In the Temple, there are two unexpected encounters. One is with a man called Simeon, whom Luke describes as 'righteous and devout, looking forward to the consolation of Israel' (Luke 2:25), that is the coming of the Messiah. He is clearly a man touched by and open to the working of the Holy Spirit, a man of alert and faithful prayer. So he recognises in this infant the arrival of God's promised saviour – not only for God's people Israel but also for the whole world. This insight he jubilantly sings out as, holding Jesus in his arms, he gives vent to that song that the Church calls the Nunc Dimittis. Though through the time of his conception and birth they have already heard some awesome things about this child, it is perhaps not surprising that, on this occasion too, Mary and Joseph 'were amazed at what was being said about him' (Luke 2:33).

There is more to come for Mary. Simeon blesses both
Mary and Joseph (which suggests he may well be a priest),
but he then turns his attention just to Mary. What he says to
her introduces a new dimension into what has already been
shared about the vocation of her son and its implications for
her as his mother. Thus far, the emphasis in the revelations
brought by the angels has been on the exalted calling of this
messianic child ('He will be great . . .', as Gabriel declared in
Luke 1:32). Now Simeon expresses something of what this
greatness might mean in human terms. Jesus will, in fact,
bring dissension and provoke opposition, not least because
he will bring to light the real truth ('the inner thoughts of
many will be revealed', Luke 2:35). The clear implication is
that he will not have an easy time.

And, therefore, nor will his mother. As Simeon puts it to
Mary, 'a sword will pierce your own soul too' (Luke 2:35).
Not least at Calvary, it is going to hurt like hell.

We are not told what Mary makes of Simeon's words. She
surely stores them away. Whether she brings herself very often
to ponder directly upon them is another matter. Subsequent
events might suggest that perhaps she cannot. Dealing with
hard words is never easy.

There is another encounter in this eventful visit to the
Temple – with the elderly prophet Anna. We shall look at
Anna a little later. Suffice to say now that she, too, recognises
the infant Jesus as who he truly is and, full of praise, shares
that not just with Mary and Joseph but also with all those
around her who are looking for God to act.

After all this, Luke tells us that Mary and Joseph return
to Galilee, to their own town of Nazareth. There, 'the child
grew and became strong, filled with wisdom; and the favour
of God was upon him' (2:39, 40). Mary no doubt has her

part to play in enabling this positive development. But when Jesus is 12 years old, she herself is to have another significant learning experience.

A child lost and found (Luke 2:41-52)

At the end of this episode in Jerusalem, Luke tells us that 'his mother treasured all these things in her heart' (2:51). From what we already know of Mary from Luke's Gospel, we are not, perhaps, surprised to hear this. But on this occasion she has really been through the mill by the time she gets to this point. She has learned that things to treasure can be quite costly.

As faithful and observant Jews, Mary and Joseph go every year to the Passover festival in Jerusalem. Passover is that great festival when the people of God remember how God delivered their ancestors from slavery in Egypt, a pivotal moment in Jewish history. On this particular visit, Mary's child has reached the age of 12 and is now, therefore, according to the beliefs of his people, on the edge of religious adulthood. He is, as it were, coming into his own – beginning to explore for himself the faith in which he has been reared and, in relation to that, his own calling in life. Mary will have to come to terms with that. Many mothers, in their own contexts, will recognise and resonate with her experience.

As is the custom, Mary, Joseph and Jesus are travelling, not as a small nuclear family unit, but as part of a much larger family and community group – a band of pilgrims all enjoying this festival experience together, looking out for one another. This being the case, it comes as less of a surprise that it takes Mary and Joseph a day's journey to discover that Jesus is not with them on their way home. Then begins a frantic search.

We can only imagine what is going through Mary's mind as she and Joseph search with great anxiety for the missing Jesus. He is not to be found among their relatives and friends. What on earth could have happened to him? They rush back to Jerusalem, by implication through the dangers of the night. All kinds of possible scenarios must be flashing through Mary's consciousness. She is no doubt also accusing herself. Why did she not keep a closer eye on him? For her, too, there must be an added dimension. All those years ago it was made clear to her that, in a special sense, this is *God's* child. And now she has lost him. She has lost the subject of her pondering and that which she treasures in her heart. She has lost her – and God's – beloved son. This loss, in all its dimensions, must be devastating.

And when at last Jesus is found safe and well, all that has been swirling around within her has to find an outlet: 'Child, why have you treated us like this?' (Luke 2:48).

Clearly, she does not understand his answer. But she must have picked up the note of implied rebuke in his words: 'Why were you searching for me? Did you not know that I must be in my Father's house?' (Luke 2:49). Those 12 years of pondering should have taken her to the Temple straightaway, not after three panic-filled days looking everywhere but the dwelling-place of God. She should have known where to find the son of God. Yet even when faced with this by Jesus himself, the penny does not drop.

Even so, Mary's response is typical. She does not understand. She is no doubt hurt and wrung out by the experience she has gone through. But she nonetheless 'treasured all these things in her heart' (Luke 2:51). She allows the word of Christ to dwell in her richly (see Colossians 3:16), even when it is not easy to take in, let alone congenial. So her relationship with her son and her Lord develops and deepens – and continues to do so, even when it *breaks* that heart in which she stores her treasure.

This is also a challenge to and for us. Especially in times of loss, times when it is hard to understand, times of anxiety and fear, Mary can encourage us to hold, somehow, to the truth of God's love – to trust, underneath it all, in the depths of our heart, that God is still with us, even when we feel we have lost him. We may then, at some stage, discover the reality of what the Lord said to Peter in another context: 'You do not know now what I am doing, but later you will understand' (John 13:7) – fruit, perhaps, of often painful pondering.

Hard words (Luke 8:19-21 and 11:27, 28)

When Mary's son grows up, he enters wholeheartedly into that divine calling which has been his since conception – to bring to all and sundry the presence, grace and challenge of the living God. It is a demanding and, as it turns out, highly dangerous mission. It is not based on force or coercion but on the determined love of God. So Jesus, by his person, his teaching and his works, presents people with God's truth and invites a response.

The response which comes (then as now) varies greatly. Many, it seems, are fascinated by Jesus. They can't get enough of his words and his works. He is, as we might say today, something of a celebrity. He attracts quite a following. But he does not change their lives, and when his behaviour no longer fits their expectations, many turn against him or simply fall away. Fans can be fickle. Others are intrigued by Jesus and do their best to understand. Yet others, the religious authorities being prominent among them, become increasingly and overtly hostile. Ominously, in human terms, these are the ones with significant power.

Few are those who stick their necks out, committing to Jesus and his message regardless of the consequences.

For Jesus, his mission must have been a lonely and hazardous path to tread. And there are more than a few hints in the Gospel records that he has to face many a temptation to veer from that path. It is clear that his struggle is not just with the vagaries of human response and opposition but also with spiritual forces of darkness and evil. Jesus knows he has to stand firm, whatever the cost. It is far from easy and it often hurts deeply.

It is in this context that we should engage with the hard words of Jesus regarding his family, uttered during his public ministry. Like the other Synoptic Evangelists, Matthew and Mark, Luke records an occasion when Jesus brusquely repels an attempt by 'his mother and his brothers' to get through to him and (as they think, for his own good) put a stop to his ministry. We shall look more closely at this episode when we explore Mark's presentation of the mother of Jesus.

For now, we shall consider an incident recorded only in Luke's Gospel, which has a very similar dominical 'punchline' to the occasion mentioned above (see Luke 11:27, 28). Jesus has been casting out demons, and this activity of exorcism, like his teaching, is provoking a divided response. Many are 'amazed' (Luke 11:14), but some accuse him of being in league with the devil. Such a dreadful misinterpretation draws from Jesus a strong and challenging response. What is at stake here is no less than the truth and goodness of God, as, in Jesus, they stand against the insidious forces of evil. This is no mere religious debating point. It is a matter of life and death.

As Jesus is engaging in this critical exchange with his opponents, a woman in the crowd raises her voice (she is determined to make herself heard) in praise of his mother. She is clearly taken with Jesus, and her way of expressing that is to say, in effect, how wonderful it must be for a mother to have produced such a son. She uses womanly, not to say maternal, imagery to convey her admiration: 'Blessed is the womb that bore you and the breasts that nursed you!' (Luke 11:27), she cries out. In that sentiment, she is, of course, echoing what has already been said by key figures in Luke's nativity narrative. The angel Gabriel declared that Mary was highly favoured by God (Luke 1:28, 30). Mary's kinswoman Elizabeth, filled with the Holy Spirit, exclaimed 'with a loud cry' when Mary went to see her, 'Blessed are you among women, and blessed is the fruit of your womb' (Luke 1:41, 42). And Mary, herself, in her great Magnificat outburst, said exultantly 'Surely, from now on all generations will call me blessed' (Luke 1:48).

So when the grown-up Jesus hears this positive voice extolling his mother, we would expect him to gladly endorse what is being shouted out. The fact that he does not unequivocally do so comes as something of a shock. His response is ambivalent, to say the least: 'Blessed rather are those who hear the word of God and obey it!' (Luke 11:28). It is hardly a resounding 'amen' to the anonymous woman's exclamation. Luke's Greek rendering of Jesus' words is in itself ambiguous. It can be taken to mean either that Jesus disagrees with the woman as to his mother's blessedness or that, while agreeing that his mother is indeed blessed, he wants to add others to that category or to issue some kind of corrective to the woman's understanding of 'blessedness'. On balance, the latter interpretation would seem to be the most likely.

The woman in the crowd, it seems, is seeking to accord both Jesus and his mother with what we might now call 'celebrity status'. They are 'A-listers', whose vocation is to receive adulation (or opprobrium) and the unremitting scrutiny of the fascinated, the curious and those out to remove such folk from their pedestals. Not so, says Jesus. They are truly blessed who respond with obedience to the word of God. It is about commitment to God's truth through thick and thin, responding to God's steadfast love with an answering unconditional love. It can take you anywhere – even to Calvary. It is not about standing on the sidelines throwing bouquets or brickbats. It costs not less than everything, but its reward is beyond price.

For Jesus, this is what being blessed by God means. His mother certainly responded with obedience at the outset of his life. So she brought him into the world and nurtured him through his formative earliest years. We should surely assume that Jesus recognised and was profoundly grateful for that. But in recent times (see Luke 8:19-21), even his mother (for the best of motives) has tried to draw him away from the ministry to which God has called him. She is no doubt trying to protect him from harm. But Jesus has to resist her misguided attempt. He has to do the work God has given him to do, whatever the consequences. Mary, like Jesus' chosen disciples, has to learn that lesson. So do we. Jesus is not our possession. We need to be under his direction, not the other way round. Therein lies the way to blessedness – even for his mother.

The Upper Room (The Acts of the Apostles 1:12-14)

The final glimpse which Luke gives us of Mary comes not in his Gospel but at the beginning of his second volume, the Acts of the Apostles. After the Ascension of Jesus, his followers gather together in an upstairs room in Jerusalem, where some of them are staying. It may well be the same room in which Jesus shared a last supper with his disciples before his death (see Luke 22:7-13). Here, we are told, the remaining 11 disciples (Judas Iscariot, who betrayed Jesus, was of course no longer among them) 'were constantly devoting themselves to prayer, together with certain women, including Mary the mother of Jesus, as well as his brothers' (Acts 1:14).

After all she has been through, she is still there, and she is still praying. The excruciating death of her son has not in any sense finished her off. Luke is silent now about Mary's responses. We can only guess at what the events of Holy Week have done to her as a mother and as a faithful believer. Any 'pondering' she has managed to do must have torn her apart. On the dreadful face of it, the rejection and execution of Jesus was a total and heartbreaking denial of all the angel Gabriel had promised. And any remembrance of her Magnificat song must have taunted her with its evidently misplaced naivety. Yet here she is, shortly after that terrible time, not huddling for comfort with her son's erstwhile followers and friends, but joining them in a prayer regime which is clearly full of hope and expectation. She has taken in the reality of the Resurrection, whether by direct contact with her risen son (the New Testament gives no indication of such an encounter but an early tradition does) or by believing the testimony of those to whom Jesus appeared after he rose from the dead. Either way, she has come to believe and trust that Jesus is alive again – and that God's promises will, after all, be fulfilled, albeit in most surprising fashion. But this time of turbulence and transition surely cannot be easy for her.

However gifted Mary may have been at pondering, there is no way that as a human being and a mother she could have gone through such a trauma without being caught up in a maelstrom of anguish. Yet by the grace and resurrection power of God, she has emerged from it. And she has done so, it seems, with a renewed faith in God and as part of a new spiritual family. She is now an integral part of the company of believers – and Jesus is now not just her son but her Lord. As such, he is the bearer and deliverer of God's promises.

One of the most immediate of those promises was given by the risen Jesus to the disciples at the time of his Ascension. It was, to put it mildly, quite a promise: 'you will receive power when the Holy Spirit has come upon you; and you will be my witnesses in Jerusalem, in all Judea and Samaria, and to the ends of the earth' (Acts 1:8). This astounding pledge is all the more surprising when we remember that the people to whom it was made all failed Jesus miserably when it came to the crunch. It is to forgiven failures, energised by the Spirit, that God entrusts this great missionary enterprise.

Mary is among the gathering of disciples in that Jerusalem upstairs room, prayerfully waiting to be endued with power from on high. She will soon experience a second 'overshadowing' of the Holy Spirit. The operation of the Holy Spirit through her body brought the body of Jesus into the world all those years ago. Now that same Spirit will shortly transform the unlikely material of his followers into a different expression of his body. The Church will shortly be born – the body of Christ charged with spreading the saving love of God throughout the world.

On what part Mary played in that, and indeed on anything that might have happened to her after Pentecost, the canonical New Testament remains silent. Other traditions abound, but we will leave her, as Luke does, in that upper room – prayerfully attentive as ever, though now, surely, with a profounder if hard-won understanding of the ways of God.

She has been on quite a journey. By her example, she can help us on ours.

Matthew's portrait of Mary (Matthew 1:18–2:23)

In Matthew's account of the birth of Jesus, Mary is very much seen but not heard. She is named, and so has her own identity, but her importance lies not in who she is or how she deals with her circumstances but in the fact of her being the mother of Jesus. She matters because she brings Jesus the Messiah into the world. Other than this, in Matthew's portrayal we get very little sense of Mary's character and responses. It is Joseph, her betrothed and then her husband, who is more to the fore. It is he who receives divine communication from angels, through the medium of dreams. And he it is who responds with obedience to what he is told. Mary, as it were, follows his lead.

In this presentation, she is spoken about and, in every sense, spoken for, but she has no direct voice of her own. We are given no idea as to how she feels about her traumatic experience. Even the reality of her pregnancy is distanced from her in Matthew's narrative – 'she was found to be with child from the Holy Spirit', we are informed. Like the verb used here, Mary is presented in passive rather than active mode. Presumably she first discovered her pregnancy for herself, but what matters in this account is its public disclosure, something that puts her in danger of shameful public humiliation, if not worse. The formal penalty for a betrothed woman found to be in Mary's condition was death by stoning (though under the terms of the Roman occupation, a death penalty should not have been carried out). Mary's predicament is serious indeed, but we can only imagine how it might have affected her.

And then there are the circumstances of her child's birth and early infancy, notably the visit of the wise men ('magi' or astrologers) from the east. Mysterious, exciting and intriguing as this must have been, it has dire consequences, triggering King Herod's paranoid cruelty. Joseph is ordered by an angel of the Lord to take the child and his mother and flee to Egypt forthwith. He does so and they flee through the night, refugees from a murderous regime. In this desperate flight, Mary shares the experience of so many mothers down the centuries, even to our own day. And she surely shares their feelings.

Does she question why God sent the wise men in the first place? If they had not come she would have been spared this nightmare – and many mothers in Bethlehem would still have their babies. Their 'wailing and loud lamentation' (Matthew 2:18) also reverberates down the ages, as well as (it must be hoped) around the throne of grace. The saving mission of God, it seems, is not without its cost, and for other innocents as well as for Jesus.

For Matthew, all the circumstances surrounding Jesus' birth make for the fulfilment of God's purposes in sending the world's Saviour – a conviction confirmed by what he found in the existing Scriptures of the people of God (hence all the quotations he includes in his narrative). One cannot help speculating that, had Luke been telling this tale, it would have prompted his Mary to engage in no little pondering and questioning.

However that may be, Matthew's Mary still has much to say to us, though it be only by implication. In carrying out her hazardous vocation, she is clearly protected and provided for by God, not least through her 'righteous man', Joseph. God's providential hand is on all her experiences. And Mary simply gets on with it, doing the work of God through her body and her obedience. Though she has much to lose – certainly her reputation, possibly her life and, as events unfold, even her child – she quite literally follows through all that is asked of her. This is clearly a woman of strong faith and trust. Even through her silence, she speaks volumes.

Mary appears once more in Matthew's Gospel, though not this time named (Matthew 12:46-50). She features in a challenging incident, which is also recorded by Luke and Mark. We shall look at it through Mark's eyes.

Mark's portrait of Mary (Mark 3:21-35; 6:1-6)

If we only had Mark's account to go on, our impression of Mary would perhaps be somewhat different. She only makes a couple of brief appearances and they are solely in relation to Jesus as an adult. And she is not presented in an entirely positive light.

It is important, however, to look at Mark's portrait of Mary in the context of the way he approaches his Gospel as a whole. One striking feature, for example, is his 'warts and all' presentation of all those close to Jesus. Far from being glossed over, their shortcomings and failures are starkly highlighted. The mother of Jesus is no exception to this pattern. Her less than helpful behaviour comes at a critical stage in Jesus' ministry, and this is underscored by the way Mark presents the episode.

Mark's Gospel is full of what scholars call 'Markan sandwiches' – significant episodes framed by briefer but equally significant incidents. The passage where Mark first mentions Jesus' mother

(Mark 3:21-35) supplies an interesting, if somewhat bitter, example. Here, the outer slices present us with a family trying to save one of their own (Jesus) from what they perceive to be his madness (what we might these days describe as mental health issues). The filling of this narrative sandwich is even more unpalatable. A delegation from the central religious establishment in Jerusalem accuses Jesus of being in thrall to the devil.

This is strong stuff. It is quite hard to swallow, let alone inwardly digest. What are we to do with it? The first thing to register is that this material, tough though it is, is meant for our nourishment. It is meant to feed our faith. We are, indeed, to 'read, mark and *learn*' from it (in the words of the old Prayer Book collect for the Second Sunday in Advent). And one of its main lessons is to alert us to the character and strategies of the spiritual opposition.

Mark is particularly stark about the workings of the enemy – and equally clear as to who has the authority and the victory. But how insidious and cutting and divisive is that enemy – here, shockingly, using as agents those on whom the Lord should be able to rely, for both recognition and strong support – his family, mentioned here for the first time in Mark's narrative, and then only once more in a passing reference (Mark 6:3). Far from encouraging him in his mission, they actively seek to undermine it. As they see it, of course, they are trying to protect him from harm – and no doubt also aiming to protect the family's reputation (a very important factor in that age and culture, as it still is, of course, in some settings). The language Mark uses of their attempt to divert Jesus from his course is strong meat. They set out to seize Jesus – to take hold of him by force so that they can keep him within the confines of their own defining.

They are convinced that he has 'lost it', gone mad with all that religious zeal (and Mark's use of the Greek imperfect tense here makes it clear that this is not just a one-off reaction on their part but an ongoing conviction).

And this is his family – including his own mother. She and his other kinsfolk misread and misunderstand him, even if for the best of motives. And the enemy readily seizes upon that to try to subvert the mission of God. If he is to stay true to the will of God, Jesus must therefore keep his loved ones at arm's length and not allow himself to fall into their hands. We can only imagine how much that must have hurt both Jesus and, in family terms, his nearest and dearest. Yet God's will is primary – even though it brings unexpected and undesired disturbance. It can shake a family to its roots. But if the kinsfolk of Jesus can bring themselves to see beyond their natural concerns and take the risk of committing to Jesus whatever, they will indeed become part of the Lord's true family – the ever-widening circle of those who seek to do God's will.

Among those, perhaps even prominently among those, we might expect to see the spiritual leaders of God's people. Sadly, however, that is not always the case. And the consequences are dire. The example with which we are presented in this episode is truly terrifying. Those entrusted with spiritual authority, from the very heart of the central religious establishment, accuse Jesus of being possessed by the powers of evil. 'He has Beelzebul, and by the ruler of the demons he casts out demons' (Mark 3:22). Ironically, as Mark has already told his audience, the demons themselves recognise Jesus for who he really is: 'Whenever the unclean spirits saw him, they fell down before him and shouted, "You are the Son of God!"' (Mark 3:11).

How could those trained and experienced scribes get it so wrong? There are no doubt many and various reasons, but among them, surely, is a resistance to acknowledging that God might work outside their rigid religious structures, along with a real sense of threat to their carefully guarded power. With such material, the enemy could and does have a field day. And that results in the commission of the ultimate sin – asserting that the Son of *God* is possessed and motivated by evil – that *God* is the very devil. No darker perversion of truth could there be. It is a vision of hell. The path that leads from fixed ideas and aggressive defensiveness can be very dangerous indeed.

Mark's Gospel does not spare us these awful realities. In fact, when we take his work as a whole, things seem to get ever bleaker. Not only is Jesus misunderstood and undermined by his own family; not only is he painfully attacked by the spiritual leaders of God's people; but he cannot even rely on the new family he has gathered around him. So, at the high point of Caesarea Philippi, he has to say even to *Peter*, his chief disciple, 'Get behind me, Satan!' (Mark 8:33).

By the time Jesus enters into the darkness of Golgotha, he is completely alone – betrayed and abandoned by his closest, chosen disciples, with even the women 'looking on from a distance' (Mark 15:40). Worse, as it feels to Jesus, even God himself, the God whom he has served unswervingly for the whole of his life, has gone away. Yet the powers of darkness are all too present. Here is the one who in every respect has done the will of God, fighting a hellish battle alone.

Mark's account allows for no softening concessions. The situation *is* utterly intolerable – yet Jesus *bears* it. And with that should come the first glimmer of hope. We remember how Mark opens his Gospel: 'The beginning of the *good news* of Jesus Christ, the Son of God' (Mark 1:1, italics added). Mark firmly believes that what might certainly be read as a narrative of gathering gloom is actually a good news story.

How so? Because Jesus the Son of God, in bearing all this, has taken on the dark forces opposed to God's will and has prevailed. Whatever strategies the enemy has employed, even using his own close family and disciples, Jesus has proved stronger. Here, says Mark, is a God you can trust, even when it feels as if all hell has been let loose against you. Whatever it feels like, God will not abandon you, though all others may. So look to Jesus, says Mark, and see the scarred yet victorious face of *God*. Take your cue from the centurion, that complete outsider who in the course of duty has just put Jesus to death. *Facing* Jesus, at the very moment when death and desolation seem to have won the day, he recognises the very presence of God (Mark 15:39).

The strong man has indeed been bound by a stronger one (Mark 3:27) – and by the most surprising and shocking of means. *God's* strategy is disarming in every sense. Therein is *our* salvation. Therein is our steadfast hope. And though we have to look elsewhere than in Mark to discover this, it seems that Mary and at least some others of Jesus' close family come to embrace its truth. Misunderstanding and its unfortunate consequences are not the end of the story for them. According to the teaching of Jesus, there is a stance which is beyond redemption – wilful persistence in calling pure good the work of the devil (Mark 3:28-30). Those who engage in this extreme exclude themselves from grace. But his family's well-intentioned mistake in, as they thought, trying to protect Jesus certainly does not fit into that category. Getting the wrong end of the stick can be, and often is, the prelude to a whole new understanding of truth.

John's portrait of the mother of Jesus
(John 2:1-12; 19:23-27)

John's Gospel provides us with two highly significant glimpses of the mother of Jesus. One comes at the beginning of her son's public ministry and the other at the end of his life. Both shed light not only on the character of his natural mother but also on the character of Jesus and the nature of discipleship more generally. Like John's Gospel as a whole, these two episodes provide us with rich material for theological reflection.

Let us start with what seems like the end.

There is no worse experience for a mother than to watch her child die. Bone of her bone, flesh of her flesh; brought to birth with much pain and struggle, water and blood; brought forth from her into a world shot through with beauty and brutality. When that which is born of her dies, it is, in many senses, death for her, too.

So it must be for the mother of Jesus, watching the fruit of her womb tortured out of existence. So it is with mothers down the ages in those many places where human life is sacrificed to the compulsive pursuit of power and vengeance. The blood of countless sons and daughters cries out to God from the ground. On the cross, God incarnate makes that cry his own. And his earthly mother watches. Here is a scene far removed from indulgent sentimentality or escapist piety. Here is a scene thoroughly at home in the horrors of our own time.

And yet, for the fourth Evangelist, the keynote of this scene is not despair but hope. As he so rightly perceives and proclaims, death and birth are very close. An end can be a beginning. Pain can issue in joy. Tragedy can give birth to triumph. That is certainly his view of Golgotha, 'the place of a skull'. 'In the place where he was crucified,' says John, 'there was a garden . . .'

(John 19:41). The place of death becomes a place of fruitfulness and renewal of life. The place of cruel extermination becomes the locus of a whole new order of creation – a new genesis, a new beginning in a new and better Eden.

It is against this background that we should seek to explore the significance of the mother of Jesus in the fourth Gospel. The Evangelist has a reason for all that he includes in his presentation – and it is not simply to record interesting events: 'These [things] are written so that you may come to believe that Jesus is the Messiah, the Son of God, and that through believing you may have life in his name' (John 20:31). All that we encounter in John's Gospel is intended to nurture that faith and life which are born of Jesus. The mother of Jesus has a telling part to play in this process – as, indeed, have a number of women given a prominent place in John's Gospel. It is not without interest and importance that again and again in this Gospel it is women who recognise and respond to the truth of Jesus. In this respect, they stand in marked and surprising contrast to the male religious establishment ('the Jews') and to the general record of the male disciples. For example, in their different ways, the Samaritan woman and Mary Magdalene go and tell others of the transforming perceptions issuing from their meetings with Jesus. Martha confronts Jesus with honest, hurting challenge – and breaks through to the kind of Christological confession that in the other Gospels is reserved for Peter. Her sister Mary proclaims in deeply moving body language the powerful reality of a love beyond words.

And then there is the mother of Jesus. She appears in person but twice in the narrative – at the Cana wedding feast, when the 'hour' of Jesus (an important emphasis in the fourth Gospel) is just beginning to dawn, and at the cross, when that hour reaches its climax. She is thus involved with 'the first of his signs' (John 2:11). 'Sign' is John's word of choice for what the other Gospels describe as Jesus' 'acts of power': they point to the truth of God. She is also involved with the last and greatest sign – that of the crucifixion. At both points she participates in beginnings and endings, endings and beginnings. At Cana, Jesus has to cross over a boundary, from his former hiddenness to a public ministry; from the gestation of a vocation to its birth. And the process is clearly not a comfortable one, as his sharp response to his mother graphically indicates – in effect, 'What's it to do with me?' At Golgotha, the ending of water and blood produces a new beginning far beyond all imagining. And the mother of Jesus is there.

She is not named (which is interesting in a Gospel full of names); neither is she addressed as 'mother' by Jesus. At the beginning and at the end he speaks to her as 'Woman'. Their relationship has much broader and deeper significance than just the natural tie of blood. This 'woman' is a paradigm of discipleship, a pointer to the character of that faith and life which flow from relationship with Jesus. Their relationship is based on blood and birth, but it has broken out of those confines in such a way as to show what relationship with Jesus can mean for all of us. So what we see in this woman can have a bearing on our own pilgrimage.

What, then, do we see? More, perhaps, the more we look. One evident trait of her character is that she stays around and perseveres against all the odds.

We see this at the Cana wedding feast where she is rudely rebuffed by the one to whom she has given so much, the one who, she knows, *could* do something to help. She refuses to take 'no' for an answer when her intuitive awareness, fruit of close relationship, tells her that 'yes' is the truth of the matter. And she takes the risk of acting on her conviction: 'Do whatever he tells you,' she tells the servants, even though Jesus has apparently made clear to her that the unfortunate lack of wine is none of their business (John 2:4, 5). Her perception turns out to be right. By her approach to Jesus, she has touched him on the raw and provoked him into (reluctantly?) accepting that his 'hour' has indeed come – that he now has to take on the ministry God has prepared for him.

That ministry leads him to the cross. No wonder he was disturbed at Cana by the woman who was at that point God's holy irritant. We see her now, standing alongside him when all seems hopeless. She does not avoid this awful situation. She does not run away. She looks straight into the face of her pain. She stands by the one to whom she is committed by heart. The fourth Evangelist does not present us with that picture of a distraught, fainting mother, familiar from so much religious art. He presents this mother, and the other friends at the scene, as standing there in faithful support – a foil to the callousness of the soldiers doing their job.

This woman, then, perseveres and is faithful, however much it hurts. She takes risks and she doesn't run away from a painful relationship. And at the cross, her very presence draws out from Jesus, *in extremis*, a final provision (John 19:26, 27).

Her behaviour and its effects stem from the depth and quality of her relationship with Jesus. In the fourth Gospel's portrait, they clearly know and understand one another at a deep level – even when there is manifest tension and hidden inner pain. It can't have been an easy relationship (far from it!), but it was undoubtedly one of fruitful tenacity and commitment, based on a love so deeply rooted that it could not be endangered by changes in surface conditions.

It is this kind of relationship that Jesus wills for the woman who is his mother and the disciple whom he loves (also not named): 'Woman, here is your son . . . Here is your mother' (John 19:26, 27). Two precious individuals are provided for – but the significance of this exchange is far greater than their particularity. It points to the way things should be between all the friends and supporters of Jesus, then and now. It is a visual cameo of how his friends should relate after Jesus has gone away – the kind of life given such emphatic prominence during the last discourses of Jesus with his disciples on the night before his death (John 13–17), a life lived in and for the love of God. For here is a relationship of equality and mutuality, of giving and receiving by both parties. It involves submission, support and service on both sides. The woman and the man are given to each other and, by clear implication, bidden to care for one another. It is by no means a one-way traffic in care – the strong man propping up the weak and helpless woman. They are both in need of strength and love. Their vocation is to minister that strength and love to each other.

Theirs is a new relationship. It is not defined by legalities or by the ties of natural kinship. Its character is that of family love at its best, but it springs out of a 'new commandment', a commandment not based on human birth or legal obligation but on the will and example of God. The parties in this relationship have been brought together by the death of God enfleshed. In so many ways, this death *is* also a birth, not least in the bringing forth of a new order of relating. Like the couple at the cross, we are given to one another by Jesus, bound in love through his death – a death which, with blood and water, releases the potential for that life which is life indeed.

If, of course, we want it. And there indeed is the rub. In Christian theory and verbiage it is all very wonderful. Christians pray about it and sing about it all the time. The reality is often a very different matter. We would rather God had not brought us together with some of our fellow disciples. And our human nature is not yet 're-created' enough for us to easily avoid the deadly clutches of the search for dominating power. How deadly and subtle those clutches are! This false god of domination is, after all, a master of disguise. Yet there is nothing more destructive of the tender plant of love.

We have arrived where we started in this reflection – love and hope trampled on by the cruel jackboots of human sin. Bitter ending. It is indeed the experience of many.

Yet the cross remains; a bloody sign of life born out of death, of joy born out of pain, of hope born out of hopelessness.

Standing by the cross is the mother of Jesus. She, too, stands there as a sign: a pointer for our pilgrimage; a woman to watch.

C. Elizabeth (Luke 1:5-80)

We have already encountered Elizabeth in our reflection on Mary's visit to her after the Annunciation. Let us now focus on her a little more closely.

She is clearly a strong and faithful woman (perhaps it runs in the family!). We only know of her from Luke's Gospel, where she plays a key role in his account of the birth of John the Baptist, the forerunner of Jesus the Messiah. John is Elizabeth's son, a longed-for surprise, who turns out to be even more surprising than at first thought.

Elizabeth is in some way related to Mary (and therefore to Jesus), but it is not made clear what the precise relationship is.

The Greek word used in Luke 1:36 to convey the angel's message simply means a female relative – hence the translations 'kinswoman' and 'relative' in the RSV and NRSVA respectively. But related Elizabeth and Mary certainly are, and by implication their *personal* relationship is close and well nurtured. They seem to be very much, as we might say, on the same wavelength. It is to Elizabeth that Mary goes 'with haste' after Gabriel's momentous visit, and their meeting suggests that they are profoundly and intuitively in tune, not least spiritually. Surely they have already shared much and deeply before this exultant encounter. Whatever their natural kinship, they are undoubtedly soul sisters.

Elizabeth is married to a priest called Zechariah, and we are told that she, too, is a descendant of Israel's foundational priest, Aaron (thus, it is interesting to note, making it distinctly possible that Mary is also). Fittingly, she shares her name with the wife of Aaron (Exodus 6:23). Both Elizabeth and her husband are described as 'righteous before God, living blamelessly according to all the commandments and regulations of the Lord' (Luke 1:6). They are clearly a most devout and faithful couple. But there is also an emptiness in their life which must have caused much grief and questioning. 'They had no children,' Luke tells us, 'because Elizabeth was barren, and both were getting on in years' (Luke 1:7).

This would be difficult enough just in human terms. To be involuntarily childless and to long for a child brings pain and desolation that defies verbal definition. Across the ages, so many have found this to be so. But for Zechariah, and perhaps particularly for Elizabeth, there is an added dimension which must be at least as challenging to bear. For a married couple to have no children is regarded in their belief culture as literally a disgrace, a sign that God's gracious favour is for some reason being withheld or withdrawn. How much this must have added to their ongoing distress. Elizabeth and Zechariah are patently faithful to God and God's law. Yet somehow they seem to be out of favour with God.

No doubt they would be praying much about it. Perhaps Elizabeth thinks of those significant women in her tradition who went through a similar experience, women like Sarah, Rachel and Hannah. We can only imagine her spiritual struggle. Barrenness blights the whole of her life and the way her community regards her. She does all she can to honour, serve and worship God. Why has God closed his ears and shut her womb?

Then the seemingly impossible happens. The news is brought by an angel, not to her (contrast Mary), but to her husband in the course of his priestly duties. Zechariah is quite literally dumbfounded by the experience, understandably finding the news hard to believe. But it duly comes to pass. Elizabeth conceives. Her response, not surprisingly, is at first cautious. She keeps it to herself until the truth of it becomes overtly evident. Then she can allow herself to release the relief and rejoicing welling up within her, even as the child takes shape in her womb. At last God has smiled on her. 'This is what the Lord has done for me,' she says, 'when he looked favourably on me and took away the disgrace I have endured among my people' (Luke 1:25). That speaks volumes.

And when Mary comes to see her, the Holy Spirit, as it were, goes into overdrive. The Spirit-filled Elizabeth – no caution here! – 'exclaimed with a loud cry':

'Blessed are you among women, and blessed is the fruit of your womb. And why has this happened to me, that the mother of my Lord comes to me? For as soon as I heard the sound of your greeting, the child in my womb leapt for joy. And blessed is she who believed that there would be a fulfilment of what was spoken to her by the Lord.'

Luke 1:41-45

With her hyper-receptive spiritual antennae, Elizabeth recognises the enormity of what God is up to and gives vent accordingly. In so many ways, not least in her untrammelled openness to the stirring of God's Spirit, Elizabeth, too, is blessed.

And when her child is born, because her husband is still voiceless, it is she who insists that the baby is given the name commanded by the angel – John, which means 'God's gracious gift'. As well as her faithfulness, she has a boldness about her. She will not give in to convention when God has directed otherwise. Though she is a woman, she will not be silenced where obedience to God is concerned.

It is indeed notable, not to say remarkable in the culture of that day, how Luke not only tells us of the vital part played by Elizabeth and Mary in God's saving mission but also enables us to hear their voices. Those voices speak eloquently about the characters of these kinswomen who are kindred spirits. And as we engage with them, we, too, find much with which to resonate. By their example and their experience, they can bring us strong encouragement, both by their humanity and their faith. So they can lead us into God's presence – a priestly vocation indeed.

D. Sisters (Matthew 13:55, 56; Mark 6:2-4. See also Matthew 12:50 and Mark 3:35)

In the Gospels of Matthew and Mark, brief, almost incidental mention is made of the sisters of Jesus. The context is the return of Jesus to his home town. On the Sabbath, Mark tells us, 'he began to teach in the synagogue, and many who heard him were astounded' (Mark 6:2). The folk among whom he had grown up found it hard to believe that this 'carpenter' (Mark 6:3) from such an ordinary family in their midst could be speaking with such wisdom and doing such extraordinary things. To them, he was not so much the local boy made good as one getting ideas above his station. Jesus was not the first or the last to discover that, as he put it, 'Prophets are not without honour, except in their home town, and among their own kin, and in their own house' (Mark 6:4).

We note that Jesus includes his own family in this pained remark. As we have seen already, at this stage in his ministry his 'kin' have not only failed to recognise his calling but also actively tried to subvert it (Matthew 12:46-50; Mark 3:31-35). They tried to restrain him, to rein him back, to take him back home where he belonged. Jesus declined to oblige. But when, later, he does voluntarily return home, it seems that he changes the minds of neither his family nor his community. It is salutary to remember that not even Jesus convinces everyone.

Among his kin there are his sisters. Whether that means they are his full blood sisters, his half-sisters, stepsisters or more distant relatives remains a matter for discussion (as it does for those termed his 'brothers'). For our purposes, what matters is that they are certainly recognised, in some real sense, as members of Jesus' family, his kin. Unlike his brothers, who are named (Matthew 13:55; Mark 6:3), his sisters remain nameless. We do not know whether they will come to believe in Jesus at a later stage. His brothers clearly will: Luke tells us they are with their mother and all the other disciples in the upper room between the Ascension and Pentecost (Acts 1:14). James becomes the leader of the Jerusalem Church. So we can perhaps speculate that at least some of his sisters eventually join the new and far wider family of Jesus – the community of those 'who hear the word of God and do it' (Luke 8:21).

In the accounts of Matthew and Mark, Jesus includes the term 'sister', as well as mother and brother, in his defining of his true family. We can only hope that the sisters in his birth family follow their mother and brothers in entering into that new spiritual reality. However that may be, the invitation to become part of Jesus' spiritual family remains open to all, ourselves included. If we do, we have the privilege of exploring what it might mean to be the sister, brother or mother of Jesus. Enormous privilege though that indeed is, it is not without its challenges. Relating to Jesus in this way brings much comfort and joy, but it also makes searching demands on the way we live our lives.

CHAPTER 3

Friends and supporters

A. Anna (Luke 2:36-38)

When we meet her in the Temple at Jerusalem, Anna the prophet is 84 years old. She was widowed when she was young, after only seven years of marriage – a recipe, if ever there was one, for despair and bitterness, for losing hope. But Anna has not taken that path. She has devoted herself to fasting and prayer, and not just on her own behalf. In her prayer, it seems, she concentrates on worshipping God and listening for God's word. She thus has developed her God-given gift as a prophet – one who can discern what God is saying and proclaim it to others. And over many long years, she has prayed with persistence and hope for the coming of God's Saviour. Having prayed so faithfully for so long, instead of giving it all up as a bad job, she is able to recognise God's moment when it finally comes.

Here indeed is a woman of deep, persevering and courageous faith. She does not let circumstances get the better of her. Instead she turns to God, prayerfully opens her life to God and lets God make of her what he will. She worships and listens and hears and speaks. She is therefore a significant example to those who come after, whatever their circumstances. Yet how easily she can be overlooked.

She is an old woman. Had she lived now, she would likely have been regarded as an 'old dear' – categorised and stereotyped out of her own unique individuality. A little old lady who can't keep away from church – a figure, more or less charitably, to poke fun at or to pity – a woman of no importance to the mainstream of life.

But she lived then. She has a *name and a meaning* – and the two are intimately related. As who she is, she has a vital role to play in the narrative of God's salvation. She is Anna, daughter of Phanuel, of the tribe of Asher. And she is a prophet.

In biblical contexts, names have a profound significance. The definitive example of that comes early in Matthew's Gospel, where the angel says to Joseph of the child to be born of Mary, 'You are to name him Jesus, for he will save his people from their sins' (Matthew 1:21). The name and its meaning are fully reflective of the child's essential identity and vocation. The name Jesus means 'God saves'.

And Anna? Anna, daughter of Phanuel, means 'God's grace, daughter of the face of God'. The 'old dear' pottering around the Temple is in truth a powerful sign of the reality of God's presence and of the way God looks at us. The face says it all (whether we like it or not). So it is, most clearly, with the face of God. On one level, seeing God's face looking at us is a fearful, terrifying prospect. Who can see God and live? How will we survive when, with no possibility of cover-up, the absolute purity of God's gaze shows us up for who we really are?

Yet on an even deeper level, we long to see God 'face to face', as Paul puts it in his famous hymn to love in 1 Corinthians 13:12. We have a profound intuition that such direct encounter will be the fulfilment of our deepest desire – the making and not the destruction of us.

That tension runs through the whole of the biblical material – but it is the positive face that most decidedly prevails. A couple of well-known examples will suffice. From the book of Numbers comes a form of blessing which we still use today:

The Lord bless you and keep you;
the Lord make his face to shine upon you, and be
  gracious to you;
the Lord lift up his countenance upon you, and give
  you peace.

Numbers 6:24-26

Seeing God's face brings an outpouring of God's grace. Grace is, indeed, the daughter of the face of God.

Many of the psalms cry out for a vision of God's face. For them, the hiding of God's face is the bleakest of prospects:

Hear, O Lord, when I cry aloud,
be gracious to me and answer me!
'Come,' my heart says, 'seek his face!'
Your face, Lord, do I seek.
Do not hide your face from me.

Psalm 27:7-9a

We note again the association between divine graciousness and the divine face.

And this from the same psalmist, who prays a prayer with which Anna would surely have identified:

One thing I asked of the Lord,
that will I seek after:
to live in the house of the Lord
all the days of my life,
to behold the beauty of the Lord,
and to inquire in his temple.

Psalm 27:4

After many years of beholding and enquiring, Anna the prophet sees at last what she has been so long looking for. In an apparently ordinary child, like so many others brought into the Temple over the years, she nevertheless perceives the gracious presence of God. She sees Jesus, and in the depths of her spirit knows immediately that he is the embodiment of that divine salvation for which she has so perseveringly fasted and prayed. She sees, to use St Paul's much later words, 'the light of the knowledge of the glory of God in the face of Jesus Christ' (2 Corinthians 4:6).

The face of a child.

Because of her determined spiritual discipline, because she fosters her God-given gifts of prophecy and prayer, Anna recognises God's moment when it comes – even though it comes in a most unexpected and surprising way. And she is then prepared to put her mouth where her faith is: 'she began to . . . speak about the child to all who were looking for the redemption of Jerusalem' (Luke 2:38). She is prepared to risk being thought a foolish old woman by sharing her conviction that here, in this ordinary little child, God has visited his people.

Her proclamation of faith will not be vindicated until years later – long after the time when she will have departed this life. But it will be a strange and shocking vindication – seen in a face which is battered and bleeding, the face of one hanging on a cross, the face of one crying out in pain and forgiveness, bearing in crucified love the sin and cruelty of the world, bearing our sin. It takes a soldier, doing his grisly job, to see it: 'Now when the centurion, who stood facing him, saw that in this way he breathed his last, he said, "Truly, this man was God's Son!"' (Mark 15:39).

But that is not the end of the matter. God's graciousness is more powerful than human viciousness. God's power to save outweighs our propensity to destroy.

God does not hide his face.

It is the face of a child.

It is the face of suffering.

It is the face of grace.

It is the face of love beyond all telling.

And at Easter, God lifts up the light of his countenance upon his Son, and breathes new life into the crucified one.

So the face of God again looks upon us, with wounded radiance. If we take the risk of turning our faces in God's direction, our faces will not be ashamed (see Psalm 34:5).

God's chosen one, God's Son, does indeed live up to his name: God saves. And an 'old dear' like Anna, daughter of Phanuel, can still point us to the redeeming graciousness of God's face. There remain many Annas – if only we will take notice of them.

B. Martha and Mary

Among the female friends and supporters of Jesus named in the Gospels, Martha and Mary are two of the most high profile. These two sisters (and their home) are clearly important to Jesus, on the level of human friendship as well as in relation to his mission. From John's Gospel we learn that they have a brother called Lazarus and that they live in the village of Bethany near Jerusalem. John also makes it clear that Jesus thinks a great deal of this sibling threesome. He loves them, we are told (John 11:5).

What we are not told, by either John or Luke (the only two Evangelists to feature the sisters), is how Jesus came to know them. That, like so much else in the life and ministry of Jesus, remains in the realm of mystery. As the end of John's Gospel puts it, 'There are also many other things that Jesus did; if every one of them were written down, I suppose that the world itself could not contain the books that would be written' (John 21:25). For both practical reasons (the limited availability of writing materials, for example) and their purposes in writing, the Evangelists needed to be selective. As regards those purposes, John helpfully spells his out, and his words, in essence, may certainly speak for the others: 'Now Jesus did many other signs in the presence of his disciples, which are not written in this book. But these are written so that you may come to believe that Jesus is the Messiah, the Son of God, and that through believing you may have life in his name' (John 20:30, 31). Everything that is included in the Gospels is meant to point us to Jesus and his significance, and to inspire faith. We need to bear that in mind when we consider all the other characters in the Gospels, Mary and Martha included. They are not presented to satisfy our (modern) curiosity about their personalities and the details of their lives. They are there to help us see Jesus more clearly. The Evangelists thus only put before us that which they consider necessary for this overriding purpose.

Within that purpose, Luke and John give us rather different perspectives on the two sisters. Yet they are recognisably the same people in both Gospels. We shall look at each Evangelist's presentation in turn.

Luke's presentation (Luke 10:38-42)

We might call it 'a tale of two women' – two women of very different character and personality, and their relationship with Jesus. Though Martha and Mary are sisters, it seems they are a bit like chalk and cheese. But both of them learn more about the character of God through this encounter with Jesus.

As indicated above, we know from what is said of them in John's Gospel that they and their brother Lazarus are close friends of Jesus. In his journeying, their house at Bethany is evidently something of a haven for him – somewhere he can relax and feel safe and at home. On this occasion, it seems he is also using it as the base for a teaching session.

Martha is determined to do the best she can for this beloved guest – to put on a good spread for a dear friend who spends a lot of time on the road and often has no leisure even to eat. She would at least make sure he has a really good meal. She hustles and bustles, driving herself to distraction. Meanwhile, her sister Mary is not lifting a finger to help. Instead of joining Martha in the proper work of the household, she is sitting at the feet of Jesus, listening to what he is saying. Martha is furious – and no doubt also extremely annoyed that she is missing out on what Mary is hearing.

Martha's personality is such that she is not backward in coming forward with her grievance. She is bold enough to interrupt Jesus while he is speaking, with both a challenge and a demand:

> 'Lord, do you not care that my sister has left me to do all the work by myself? Tell her then to help me.'
>
> *Luke 10:40*

We note how carefully Jesus responds. He does not rebuke her for what others, particularly in the culture of that time, might consider to be rudeness and temerity. ('How dare you interrupt me? How dare you speak to me like that?') He respects her feelings and what she says, but at the same time he tries to enlarge and deepen her understanding. 'Martha, Martha' (note the affectionate repetition), 'all this distracted rushing around, all this worry and stress is not good for you. Nor is it necessary. I don't need all this fuss made of me. A simple meal would have been quite ample. Then you and Mary could have sat down together with me.' That is the sense of his words in Luke 10:41, 42.

Mary has cottoned on to the wisdom of God more readily than Martha. She realises that when Jesus draws near, the priority is to take advantage of his presence and drink in his teaching. In sitting at his feet, she is adopting the usual posture of a disciple learning from their teacher. The difference is that she is a woman, and in the culture of that day, women were not supposed to be theological students! Typically, Jesus breaks with convention, making it very clear that he wants women as well as men to learn from him. The wisdom of God is there for everybody – whatever their gender, whatever their background. All that is needed is enough wisdom to listen to it.

Two women, two sisters, two very different personalities and two contrasting approaches to Jesus. Yet it is important to remember that they are both special to Jesus, they are both valued by Jesus, and they both learn something of the wisdom of Jesus – Martha by confronting him honestly and directly with her distress and frustration, Mary by sitting at his feet and quietly receiving his teaching.

Jesus responds to both in a way that shows he understands. He understands them, and he understands where they are coming from.

We can be greatly encouraged by that. There will be times when, like Martha, in the midst of great pressure, we need to say in raw honesty, 'Lord, don't you care . . . ?' There will also be times when we need to shut the door on the frantic demands of modern life, to be brave enough to follow Mary's example and simply sit at the feet of Jesus, whatever else might be going on.

God comes to us where we are. God loves us, whatever. That is one of the key messages of this domestic incident at Bethany, thankfully preserved for us by Luke the Evangelist.

John's presentation (John 11:1–12:8)

The raising of Lazarus (John 11)

In the drama which is John's Gospel as a whole, this scene propels us, in heart and mind, into the drama's final, decisive act. In that act, tragedy and triumph, humiliation and glory are painfully woven together. The encounters of Jesus with Mary, Martha and their brother Lazarus point us to the great mystery of Good Friday and Easter. They prefigure (and help provoke) the Passion and Resurrection of Jesus. They also have much to say about how God continues to meet with us, not least in the hard and heartbreaking experiences of life – and it is on this dimension that we shall focus in this reflection.

So to Martha and Mary. One of the striking features of John's Gospel is its inclusion of a number of extended, highly charged and theologically significant meetings between Jesus and women. In the culture of the time, women could neither be legal witnesses nor, as we have said, students of theology. Indeed, any public conversation between a man and a woman, let alone on a religious matter, was looked upon with great disapproval. Yet the women of the fourth Gospel bear powerful witness to Jesus – and Jesus has no hesitation in encouraging that witness. In this area, as in so many others, Jesus breaks through conventions and traditions in the interests of deeper truth.

On this occasion, Martha, too, acts unconventionally. Instead of doing the expected thing – staying in the house with her sister and their female companions, grieving for a beloved brother – she takes the initiative and goes out to meet Jesus as soon as she hears he is coming – coming at last. There are things to say to this friend who, despite urgent pleas, has failed to come when he was most needed. Some things are far more important than the norms of acceptable behaviour. Boldly and straightforwardly she confronts Jesus with how she feels: 'Lord, if you had been here, my brother would not have died' (John 11:21). So much is contained in that raw and passionate challenge. Why, Lord? Why did you not come when we asked you for help? We thought you cared about us. You've helped so many others. Why not us, your faithful friends?

Many, through the generations and down to this day, would recognise that anguished, indeed angry, prayer. Many have suppressed it. Martha tells Jesus straight. A telling example, perhaps.

Without giving Jesus space to respond to her challenge, Martha nevertheless goes on to articulate a stubborn faith that has not died with her brother. Outwardly, things might seem hopeless, but hope is still alive because of the presence of Jesus. 'But even now,' she says, 'I know that God will give you whatever you ask of him' (John 11:22). Her audacious tenacity opens up an exchange of profound and revelatory significance.

It is with determined, honest Martha that Jesus shares the heart of the world's hope: 'I am the resurrection and the life. Those who believe in me, even though they die, will live, and everyone who lives and believes in me will never die.' As she has challenged him, so now Jesus challenges Martha: 'Do you believe this?' (John 11:25, 26).

Though her brother remains dead and buried, Martha needs no further persuading. Her sparky encounter with Jesus may not have answered all her questions, but it has brought her face to face with the reality of God. Her confession of faith rivals that of Peter, recorded in the other Gospels, and is unadulterated by that disciple's subsequent denial of his Lord: 'Yes, Lord,' she says, 'I believe that you are the Messiah, the Son of God, the one coming into the world' (John 11:27).

Martha is, in all honesty, a woman of searching faith – a faith that remains in dialogue with her plentiful supply of down-to-earth common sense. That becomes clear as she stands with Jesus before the tomb of her brother. She protests when Jesus orders the stone to be taken away from the tomb entrance: 'Lord, already there is a stench because he has been dead for four days' (11:39).

That is a fair point. It needs another challenge from Jesus to rekindle her confidence: 'Jesus said to her, "Did I not tell you that if you believed, you would see the glory of God?"' (11:40). As with so many of us, Martha's faith needs ongoing boosts from the Lord.

As we see her in John's Gospel, then, Martha's world is not confined to or by the stress of the kitchen. She most definitely has a mind of her own – a mind of no mean intelligence. And Jesus respects that.

Jesus responds to people where and as they are, regardless of context and convention. With Martha, that involved a profound verbal, not to say theological, exchange. She needed to use words to express her feelings. With her sister Mary, who is overwhelmed by grief, the emphasis moves to non-verbal communication. The sight of the friend she had pinned her hope on, come at last but too late, makes her collapse in front of him in desperation. Here she sobs out the same wounded statement with which her sister had confronted Jesus: 'Lord, if you had been here, my brother would not have died' (John 11:32). They have no doubt expressed that sentiment to each other a good deal, as they endured their waiting and mourning with no sign of Jesus.

The emotional reaction of Jesus to the distress in front of him is very strong indeed. We might say, colloquially, that the situation gets to him at 'gut level': 'he was greatly disturbed in spirit and deeply moved' (John 11:33). That latter verb in Greek has connotations not just of pity but also of inner turmoil, even anger. Faced with human tragedy, Jesus is far more than sympathetic. He identifies with the sufferers, sharing their grief and feeling their anger at its cause. On a human level, is he also struggling with the fact that it was actually his own deliberate delay that plunged his friends into the agony of bereavement (John 11:1-14)? However that might be, seeing Mary his beloved friend so overcome with grief makes his own inner anguish erupt into tears. It is not the only time that he weeps. That should not, in any sense, be an embarrassment. It should, rather, be a tremendous encouragement to know that in Jesus (whom Martha rightly perceives to be the Son of God) we have one who feels in himself the confusion and heartbreak of human suffering – and can also give vent to it. That is not wimpish. It is godly.

Still in a disturbed state, Jesus goes with Mary and Martha to the tomb where Lazarus is buried. They are accompanied by those who have been consoling the sisters in their home and who followed Mary out when she responded to Martha's word in her ear that Jesus was calling for her (another sign, incidentally, of the closeness of their friendship). In all probability, in accordance with the convention of the time, most of these consolers, who then witnessed the raising of Lazarus, would have been women – another feature in which the experience of Lazarus prefigures the resurrection of Jesus. Women are the first witnesses to what has happened.

What has happened here at Bethany is breathtaking, even as it returns breath to Lazarus. Laid in the tomb, he most certainly has no power of himself to help himself. Unlike his sisters, he cannot protest and he cannot weep at his fate. All passion is indeed spent. God help him. And, indeed, God does, fulfilling the dead man's name: 'Lazarus' means 'God helps'. It is the passionate faith of Jesus that calls Lazarus out from his state of non-being in the tomb. The voice of Jesus reaches into the heart of darkness, effecting rescue when all seems utterly lost.

But for Lazarus, being saved from death is not the end of the matter. He staggers forth from the tomb still encased in his grave-clothes. He has to be released from that which prevents him from enjoying the full blessings of life. 'Unbind him, and let him go,' says Jesus (John 11:44). He says it still, in many and various ways and in many situations where people are held in thrall.

Not long after Lazarus, Jesus himself will experience the same liberation. And the first to encounter him will be another Mary weeping outside another tomb. This time, however, emergence from the tomb will be far more than a return to normal human life. For by his resurrection Jesus is let loose in all the world. He is wherever we are, waiting to meet us, calling us into newness of life. Like Martha, Mary and Lazarus, we too can know his power to save.

The anointing at Bethany (John 12:1-8)

This must have been a memorable dinner party! On the one hand it is an occasion overflowing with happiness and thanksgiving. On the other, it is an exposure of evil and a precursor of death. For Martha, Mary and Lazarus, it is a golden opportunity to express their gratitude and their joy that Lazarus has been raised from the dead and brought out of the tomb.

They all do so in different ways. Lazarus relaxes and feasts with Jesus, no doubt savouring his return to life and health – reclining at a dinner table after reclining in a tomb. True to character, Martha gets on with the practicalities that enable the feasting to happen. And Mary, also true to character, speaks volumes through an uninhibited and extravagant non-verbal gesture.

It belongs to Judas to shatter the atmosphere of heartfelt love. His mean hypocrisy is that of one unscrupulous enough to betray the trust placed in him by his friends 'Why was this perfume not sold for 300 denarii [nearly a year's wages for a labourer] and the money given to the poor?' he asks. 'He said this,' John tells us, 'not because he cared about the poor, but because he was a thief; he kept the common purse and used to steal what was put into it' (John 12:5, 6). We may wonder that Jesus, who (according to the fourth Evangelist) 'knew what was in everyone' (John 2:25), chose Judas as a disciple and bore with him for so long. God, indeed, moves in mysterious ways. In the end, Jesus will give Judas permission to go out and perpetrate his ultimate work of darkness. By that stage, Jesus will even have stooped down to wash his betrayer's feet. Even to Judas, he shows 'the full extent of his love' (John 13:1, New English Bible).

The Bethany dinner is in celebration of deliverance from death. Yet it also points to the death of the deliverer. The all-pervading fragrance of Mary's ointment is, in a profound sense, also the odour of death. Before very long, Jesus will be as dead and buried as Lazarus has been – not through physical sickness but because of the sickness of the world.

There is so much going on in this passage. It bristles with tension, impending tragedy and a love that is beyond all telling. As always in St John's Gospel, there are many layers of meaning. Let us focus here on Mary and her reckless act of devotion. Not long before, she no doubt assisted in the anointing of her brother's dead body. Now, with a large quantity of costly and fragrant ointment, she anoints Jesus.

Just as Mary reacted emotionally and largely non-verbally to her devastating bereavement, so her thanksgiving to Jesus for the raising of her brother is an extravagant and highly charged gesture that throws all caution to the wind. It is a gesture that risks serious misinterpretation. For a respectable woman, is this not going too far? It is also a gesture which, like the ointment, is heady with meaning.

In anointing the feet of Jesus and wiping them with her hair, she is, as he makes clear, prefiguring his burial. Indeed, Jesus' words could well imply that this is part of Mary's own intention, suggesting that she, at least, in 'sitting at his feet' has taken in the import of his teaching: 'Leave her alone.

She bought it so that she might keep it for the day of my burial' (John 12:7).

Mary is also anticipating something Jesus is very shortly to do for his disciples. Just as he will wash the disciples' feet, so Mary attends with love to the cleansing of *his* feet. Unlike the disciples, she doesn't need the lesson spelling out. Love says it all.

There is no mention of tears in this anointing episode (unlike the anointing in Luke 7:38-50, which we shall consider later). This is a solemn and silent act – yet one redolent with fragrance, emotion and meaning.

Not only is it a prefiguring (just as the death and raising of Lazarus is also a prefiguring) of the death and resurrection of Jesus; it is also a wordless icon of the calling of the disciple to share Christ's Passion. As St Paul puts it somewhat later:

I want to know Christ and the power of his resurrection and the sharing [literally, the communion] of his sufferings by becoming like him in his death, if somehow I may attain the resurrection from the dead.

Philippians 3:10, 11

In wiping the anointed feet of Jesus with her hair, Mary is sharing in his anointing. The ointment becomes common to them both. Just as he identified with her in her tears for Lazarus, so now she identifies with him in his impending Passion.

And all for love. There is the heart of the matter. Love indeed says it all. In many and various ways, both verbally and non-verbally, love says it all. Love speaks honestly, out of the depths. Love shows its feelings, whatever critics might think and say. Love holds on to hope.

We see that in Mary of Bethany. We see it supremely in Jesus.

C. Mary Magdalene

Mary Magdalene is one of the most attractive figures in the earliest history of the Church. It is not surprising, therefore, that all kinds of myths and legends have accrued around her – some more imaginative than others! However, what little is said about her in the New Testament record is interesting enough, and it is that on which we shall be focusing in this reflection.

From the named references to Mary in the New Testament, we learn that Jesus healed her of severe mental disturbance, after which she became one of his loyal and loving followers. Indeed, she was one of those women who, according to Luke, 'provided for them [i.e. Jesus and the disciples] out of their resources' (Luke 8:1-3). We shall look more at that in a later section (see chapter 3, section D). But we note here that there is no mention of any background in prostitution and 'loose living'. That alleged association came later by means of speculative connections. Mary's great claim to fame and lasting attention is that, according to all the Gospels, she was one of the first witnesses to the Resurrection of Jesus. Indeed, in all the Gospel accounts of Easter, she is mentioned first among the named women, a sign of her importance in the early Christian community.

Let us look now in turn at the various perspectives of the Evangelists.

Matthew's perspective (Matthew 28:1-10)

Matthew tells us that Mary was one of the 'many women' present at the crucifixion of Jesus, 'looking on from a distance' (Matthew 27:55, 56). He then informs us that

Mary Magdalene and 'the other Mary' (see chapter 3, section D) were present and 'sitting opposite the tomb' when Joseph of Arimathea buried Jesus' body (Matthew 27:61). According to Matthew, these two women visit the tomb again, as soon as they can after the Sabbath, just 'as the first day of the week was dawning' (Matthew 28:1). They clearly want to express their grief and desolation and – as we learn from the other Evangelists – to give the proper attention to his body which was not possible on that awful Friday afternoon.

What then happened is not awful but awesome, unsurprisingly filling them with fear. In Matthew's words, 'suddenly there was a great earthquake; for an angel of the Lord, descending from heaven, came and rolled back the stone and sat on it. His appearance was like lightning, and his clothing white as snow' (Matthew 28:2, 3). Though all the Evangelists mention angelic involvement in the Resurrection, only Matthew describes this seismic intervention. It terrifies the guards Pilate has set on the tomb, shocking them into unconsciousness. But Mary Magdalene and her companion are told (in typical angelic fashion) not to fear, and are given a message of equally seismic significance and encouragement:

> 'Do not be afraid; I know that you are looking for Jesus who was crucified. He is not here; for he has been raised, as he said. Come, see the place where he lay. Then go quickly and tell his disciples, "He has been raised from the dead, and indeed he is going ahead of you to Galilee; there you will see him." This is my message for you.'
>
> *Matthew 28:5-7*

They rush off to deliver this amazing message, their continuing fear now mixed with 'great joy'. It seems that against all the odds, the words of Jesus before his death have been proved true. He has been raised from the dead. The impossible has happened! And then the impossible takes shape. Jesus himself meets them – characteristically, with a warm greeting and a word to calm their fear. Understandably, their response is to fall at his feet and worship. Indeed, they take hold of those precious feet, no doubt to prove to themselves that they are not imagining things. And as they cling on for dear life, they surely see – and feel – his wounds. Typically, however, they are soon raised to *their* feet by the Lord, who reminds them, by repeating the angel's message, that there is a job to be done. As ever, worship should issue in doing God's will.

Mark's perspective (Mark 16:1-8)

Mark also tells us that Mary Magdalene was among the many women watching the crucifixion from a distance, informing us that these women 'used to follow him and provided for him when he was in Galilee' (Mark 15:40, 41). Along with Luke's similar comment, mentioned earlier, this suggests that whatever else she might have been, Mary Magdalene was a woman of means – and, it seems, an independent one. She was rich in more than emotion!

She was also utterly loyal and devoted to Jesus. His crucifixion must have been like a deathblow for her (though only John the Evangelist really spells this out). Mark's account has her coming to the tomb 'very early on the first day of the week, when the sun had risen' (Mark 16:2). She comes with Mary the mother of James and Salome (see chapter 3, section D). They bring spices, we are told, in order that they might anoint the body of Jesus. As they make their way there, they ask each other who might be found to roll away the heavy stone from the tomb entrance. It will be too much for them to manage. The fact that they have not sorted this out before setting out on their expedition says much about their state of mind and heart. (One wonders why they did not involve the male disciples, for example – or perhaps they did, and were rebuffed.) What matters more than anything, what pushes all other considerations to the margins, is to get to Jesus as soon as they can. What they want to do was out of bounds on the Sabbath day, but at first light on the day after they go with haste to the tomb, to provide for Jesus (as is their wont) even in death.

To their surprise, and no doubt consternation, they discover that the stone has already been rolled away. Surprise turns to fear when they venture into the tomb and encounter 'a young man, dressed in a white robe, sitting on the right side' (Mark 16:5). He is not described specifically as an angel, thus inevitably giving rise to subsequent speculation as to his identity. Is he, for example, the 'certain young man' of Mark 14:51, 52, who followed Jesus to the Gethsemane garden and ran off naked when Jesus was arrested (and was that young man Mark himself)? But all that is said of the young man in Mark 16 suggests that here indeed is an angel. He is dressed in a white robe, he tells the women not to be afraid, he speaks to them authoritatively and he gives them orders from the Lord. They are to go and tell the disciples (significantly here with explicit mention of Peter) the news that Jesus has been raised from the dead and, just as he told them, is going before them into Galilee – home base for Jesus and his mission. That mission is about to be renewed, and in a way which will cross all geographical boundaries.

What happens next is an ongoing subject of debate among students of Mark's Gospel. Most scholars believe that verse 8 of chapter 16 is, in fact, the ending of Mark's Gospel, whether because that is how Mark intended it, or because he was interrupted before he could finish, or because his original ending has been lost. It is not the most obvious ending for a Gospel, particularly one which has opened by saying it was telling a good news story: 'So they went out and fled from the tomb, for terror and amazement had seized them; and they said nothing to anyone, for they were afraid.'

It is not surprising that, before very long, other endings were added, seeking to make Mark's conclusion more satisfactory and more consistent with the way events turned out (see Mark 16:9-20). It seems clear from the other Gospels, and indeed from the formation of the early Church, that the angel's message was in fact delivered, Mary Magdalene taking a leading role in that, whether with others (Matthew and Luke) or singly (John). If Mark did intend to end his writing at verse 8, he must have had a good reason, which, in his view, strengthened rather than contradicted the good news of the Resurrection.

Perhaps it has something to do with the strong emphasis in his Gospel on the awe that Jesus aroused in his ministry and by his very presence. It is an awe which suggests the presence and the working of the divine. A proper response to an encounter with God is holy fear (of which the Scriptures are full of examples). The women's experience on Easter morning falls very much into this category. They are overwhelmed by the awesomeness of God's intervention, and their first coping strategy is to run away. Mark may well have simply assumed that his intended audience would be aware of the eventual outcome. It was a sense of God's mighty power, even over death, that he wanted to leave them with. What God has done in raising Jesus should arouse more fear and trembling than any human opposition believers might be facing (and the original receiving community for this Gospel may well have been facing the real threat of persecution). God is the greatest force there is.

For us, it may be salutary to be reminded of the reality of God's supernatural character and power – to be reintroduced to the dimension of awe and wonder in our faith. It is all too easy and tempting to domesticate God. Yet the Easter God is indeed awesome – and in a far stronger sense than the contemporary usage of that word.

Luke's perspective (Luke 23:55–24:11)

Luke adds some details to his Easter morning narrative which we do not find in the other Gospels. Much is the same. The early morning visit to the tomb involving Mary Magdalene, the alarming discovery that the stone has been rolled away and the tomb is empty, the encounter with angels (two in Luke) who deliver a message about Jesus being raised from the dead. But Luke enables us to see things from a slightly different angle.

His group of women, again headed by Mary Magdalene, consists also of Joanna, Mary the mother of James and 'the other women'. These women are at first 'perplexed' and 'terrified', but, unlike Mark's account, Luke's does not end there. And the angels' message to them is phrased somewhat differently: 'Why do you look for the living among the dead? He is not here, but has risen. Remember how he told you, while he was still in Galilee, that the Son of Man must be handed over to sinners, and be crucified, and on the third day rise again' (Luke 24:5-7). There is more detail here about Jesus' teaching but, even more significantly, it is the women who are told to remember it. They are not simply told to remind the men. It is assumed that they themselves have heard the teaching at first hand and it is important for them to recall it. In other words, Mary Magdalene and the others were not just suppliers of material support to Jesus and his male followers; they were themselves also disciples in receipt of his teaching – teaching moreover which was directed at his close followers rather than the wider public. As far as Jesus is concerned, they belong in the inner circle rather than on the periphery.

What the male disciples make of them is rather suggested by Luke's description of the women's reception when they tell of their experience and the angels' message: 'But these words seemed to them an idle tale, and they did not believe them' (Luke 24:11). Dismissed, no doubt, as the fanciful imaginings of overwrought and unreliable women. That must be hard for the women to take (though perhaps it does not surprise them). At least they are shortly afterwards proved right!

John's perspective (John 19:25; 20:1-18)

It is John's Gospel that perhaps offers us the best opportunity of an in-depth encounter with Mary Magdalene. John's account of her Easter experience focuses solely on her. The 'other women' of the Synoptic Gospels are not mentioned. Here we meet a woman who speaks for herself, whose experience we can enter into and, in our own way, share. She is not just named by the Evangelist, she is also named by the Lord, and the reality of her character shines through. Within the context of his narrative as a whole, John is clearly a skilled portrayer of individual persons, not least women – one of the reasons we warm to him, perhaps.

He is also a profound theologian who has reflected deeply and prayerfully on the significance of Jesus and his mission. This comes through strongly in his Gospel writing, which is intended to establish and strengthen our faith in Jesus as the Son of God, so that we 'may have life in his name' (John 20:30, 31). It is important to see John's presentation of Mary Magdalene in this light. She is not, in fact, the primary focus of attention. She points us to Jesus, who points us (to use his own words) to 'my Father and your Father, to my God and your God' (John 20:17). We need to explore this a little more if we are to fully appreciate Mary Magdalene's significance in the Gospel story.

It is John the Evangelist who brings out most clearly that, in Jesus, God has brought about a new creation. The fourth Gospel, like the book of Genesis, opens with the phrase, 'In the beginning', and it climaxes in the Easter narrative with these words: 'Early on the first day of the week, while it was still dark, Mary Magdalene came to the tomb and saw that the stone had been removed from the tomb' (John 20:1). Just as on the first day of the original Genesis, on this Paschal first day of the week there is darkness and emptiness – a great void. And when, in raising Jesus, God says afresh, 'Let there be light', as at the beginning, only God is there to witness the amazing outcome. Yet again, God's wonders have been wrought in the dark.

But this time, the darkness God has engaged with is rather more than the shadowy substance of primordial potential. This darkness is blackened with the intensity of evil and sin, of pain and suffering, of injustice and cruel death. This darkness is dark indeed – and darkness, we note, like light, is another pervasive Johannine theme. It is not surprising, then, that for the human participants in this momentous drama, it takes a while for the light to dawn. New creation there might be, but the erstwhile friends and followers of Jesus are not exactly in the best condition to take it on board. How drastically their lives have been turned upside down. All they enjoyed, all they experienced and learned, all they looked forward to in their life with Jesus – suddenly gone. It all happened so quickly, and they have little to be proud of in the way they responded. Little wonder they are confused and lost, in every sense stumbling about in the dark. And now, it seems, they have lost even his body. It surely cannot get much worse.

But the empty tomb, of course, does not signify a lost body but the outbreak of new and indestructible life. And the first person to discover this life-changing truth is the one who (unlike Simon Peter and the other disciple) does not scuttle off home when she discovers the great absence – the one who stays there, staring into the void, staring her pain and confusion, lostness and grief square in the face – Mary Magdalene.

Mary has her momentous encounter in a garden. This is not just the garden of Resurrection. As John has already tellingly stated, 'there was a garden in the place where he was crucified' (John 19:41). This new Eden is no blissful return to primal innocence. The one who has sprung up in this garden is the one who was strung up there on a tree – that tree which is both the tree of life and the tree of the knowledge of good and evil – the cross. The one who hung there is for ever marked and scarred by that tree – and his wounds are for ever tender.

This act of new creation is indeed *new*. It does not take us back to the beginning. Nor does it take us back to where we were before, much as we might desire to recapture the past. Mary has to discover that – and so, very often, do we. At enormous cost, God has done a *new* thing – something which opens up possibilities beyond our imagining – something which takes us forward into fresh understanding, new challenges and spiritual adventures of which we could hardly have dreamed.

Mary Magdalene is a focal and very personal example of Easter's new creation truth. We notice that, as with Peter a little later, though for different reasons, the risen Jesus addresses Mary three times. He recognises, it seems, that Mary needs to go on a threefold journey of healing, transformation and new commissioning. Her relationship with the Lord needs to be remade.

Each of the three dominical approaches is introduced by the Evangelist with the same phrase – literally, in English, 'Says to her, Jesus . . .' John uses the present tense to give a sense of immediacy (as we often do when we're telling a story) and to stress that what Jesus says to Mary has something to say to us *now*, in the present, in *our* present. And John puts the name of Jesus in the emphatic position at the end of the Greek phrase to make it clear that Jesus is the primary focus of attention. As Mary does eventually, it is to Jesus that we must turn and look.

The first time Jesus speaks to Mary, she has just turned away from looking into the void of the tomb and her startling vision of angels. They have not told her what she desperately wanted to know – where to find the body of her Lord – and she is still weeping with anguish and grief. Not surprisingly, perhaps, she does not recognise this further unexpected figure, even when he speaks to her. She supposes him to be the gardener (and in the truest sense, that indeed is what he is).

Jesus begins by repeating the angels' question but then takes it further: Says to her Jesus, 'Woman, why are you weeping? For whom are you looking?' (John 20:15).

He knows, of course. He knows that the emptiness of the tomb reflects the emptiness of Mary's life. He knows her state of utter hopelessness and intense personal pain – and he knows the reason for it. He knows that she stood with his mother near his cross, watching his tortured death (John 19:25). He knows what this has done to her – that she has sustained a brutal loss she can hardly bear – the loss of someone who meant the world to her, who made her well in every respect, gave her meaning and love, joy and a sense of worth – someone for whom, even now, though he is dead and gone she would do anything. But he *is* gone – and in the most agonising of circumstances. And now even his body has been taken away. There is nothing left. What hope now for the future? The prospects are bleak. Utter hopelessness. Intense personal pain.

Jesus knows all this. But he knows also that hurting feelings need to be articulated – wept out – shared – talked about. It is instructive that Jesus doesn't *tell* Mary how she is feeling, or even say that he *knows* how she is feeling. He *asks* her – and in such a way as to give her the confidence to respond honestly. There is real pastoral care and concern in the way Jesus asks, and Mary instinctively recognises that. She responds with a glimmer of hope – though not yet hope for the right thing. 'Sir,' she says, 'if you have carried him away, tell me where you have laid him, and I will take him away' (John 20:15). She does not directly answer his questions but her words express everything. Shock and grief prevent her from seeing that the desire of her heart is right in front of her, but this experience of genuine care has begun to kindle the first stirrings of hope.

So it always is with Jesus, whether we recognise him for who he is or not. The listening, caring ears of Jesus take many forms.

For Mary, the moment of amazed recognition comes when Jesus calls her by name: Says to her Jesus, 'Mary . . .' (John 20:16). That familiar affirmation of her identity and her worth is the key that unlocks the real truth. This moment is truly beyond words. We can only imagine the full reality of Mary's reaction: 'Rabbouni!' – Master – Teacher. The impossible, the unbelievable has happened! All that pain and loss gone like a bad dream.

Not so, however. The nightmare has been all too real. It cannot simply be shrugged off. It needs to become a crucial and redeemed influence on the future. Mary's Rabbouni has to gently teach her that things can no longer be as they were. Mary has to move on with her life, move on in her relationship with Jesus, move on into a much better and more fulfilling future. And through it all, Jesus will always be there for her, calling her by name. As he will for all those who come after.

Says to her, Jesus, 'Do not hold on to me, because I have not yet ascended to the Father. But go to my brothers and say to them, "I am ascending to my Father and your Father, to my God and your God"' (John 20:17).

'Do not hold on to me.' The Greek expression suggests that Mary, not unnaturally, is doing just that – clinging on to Jesus for sheer joy, for dear life! But Jesus knows that if she is going to grow into her new relationship with him, she has to let go: let go of the past, wonderful as it has been, so that she can embrace an even better future – and do the job the Lord wants her to do. What is that? To go and tell. To be God's angel, God's messenger, God's apostle. To proclaim to those locked up in fear and despair the glorious truth of Resurrection, of light bursting out of hellish darkness, of newly created life and freedom, of the ultimate triumph of the Creator's goodness.

She must share her experience. Just as she told the men about the empty tomb, so she must now share with them the joyful truth of what it means. This emotional woman, at that time disqualified by her gender from being a legal witness or a religious teacher, is nonetheless entrusted by the Lord with an essentially apostolic function. No wonder she soon becomes known as 'the apostle to the apostles'. She is to proclaim to the scared and bewildered male disciples the fact of the Resurrection and the heavenly significance of Jesus. How typical of Jesus to break down the barriers of human prejudice.

The Lord's word is not just for Mary but for all who would follow him. Jesus is not our private possession. We cannot hold on to him in that sense – to seek to hug him to ourselves and our own personal experience. Jesus is for everyone, and everyone needs to hear that. It is our duty and our joy to 'go and tell' (by the way we live, as well as in our words and actions): to tell of that divine life and love which cannot be destroyed, even by cruel death; to tell of that divine life and love which gives meaning and joy to human existence, that says to every individual in their uniqueness and whatever their circumstances, 'You matter.'

The encounter is enough. Off Mary Magdalene goes. And before she delivers the message with which she has been entrusted, she exclaims the experience that gives motive and authenticity to all her following words: 'I have seen the Lord' (John 20:18).

It is seeing Jesus which makes all the difference. Indeed, it makes all things new.

D. Supporters and providers

As we have seen in the previous sections, Mary Magdalene was one of the women who provided for Jesus and his entourage out of their own resources (Luke 8:1-3; Mark 15:40, 41). There were 'many' of them, it seems, meaning Jesus must have gone about his itinerant ministry 'through cities and villages' (Luke 8:1) accompanied by a fair number of supporters, both male and female. Perhaps this increased the sense of threat he posed to the established authorities, who were clearly rattled. Certainly it meant that more than just the 12 disciples benefited from the daily presence of Jesus, along with the teaching he aimed at his committed followers.

For these women are rather more than detached benefactors and well-wishers, making their donations from a safe distance. They give more than their money. Their response to Jesus is one of sacrificial generosity. Like the male disciples, they leave everything to follow him, contributing all that they have to his mission. That includes themselves. And in a real sense, they have more to lose than the men. They surely risk their reputations in following this man Jesus around. How the tongues must have wagged. These are clearly women of means and very probably status (certainly so in the case of Joanna, the wife of King Herod's steward Chuza). Yet they are prepared to give away their means, set aside their privileged lifestyles and risk calumny in order to support and receive the ministry of one who has no official position and who is, indeed, provoking powerful opposition as well as admiration. They are being led along a potentially very dangerous path. Who knows what those they have left behind are making of it.

Whatever their precise personal backgrounds, they obviously feel able to do what they believe is right with their 'means' and their lives. It is important to recognise the existence of such women in what was, generally, what we might call a patriarchal society. Even so, we should not underestimate the risk inherent in their sacrificial discipleship. For discipleship it is – and not just in terms of (so to speak) writing the cheques and doing the cooking and washing. Like Mary of Bethany, but in many different locations, they are there to sit at the feet of Jesus – to listen and learn.

What possessed them to do this? The person of Jesus himself, with his charismatic aura of holy authority, must have been the great draw. Luke also tells us that some of them, at least, have 'been cured of evil spirits and infirmities' (Luke 8:2). Their gratitude must have been immense, and a powerful motivation to commit themselves to the one who had given them back their lives and their dignity. Especially so, perhaps, with Mary Magdalene, 'from whom seven demons had gone out' (Luke 8:2). That phrase implies that her mental disturbance was very severe – bad enough in any era, but especially so in a context where mental illness was often regarded as the work of the devil, a view to which we would not, of course, subscribe today. But Jesus, the incarnate Son of God, who always meets us where we are, engages with the situation as it is perceived, tackling it on its own ground, and by exorcism restores Mary and many afflicted ones to health. No wonder she became so completely devoted to the one who had delivered her from such acute distress.

Some of the women, like Mary, are named by the Evangelists, presumably because they come to play a known role in the early Church. As well as Mary Magdalene (highlighted in all the Gospels), Luke mentions by name 'Joanna, the wife of Herod's steward Chuza, and Susanna' (8:3). Susanna is mentioned nowhere else in the New Testament, even in Luke's account of the women at Easter, where Joanna reappears (Luke 24:10). Mark's list of named women who travel to Jerusalem with Jesus and are present on Good Friday and Easter Day consists (in addition to Mary Magdalene) of 'Mary the mother of James the younger and of Joses, and Salome' (Mark 15:40, 41; 16:1). Matthew, in his account of the death and resurrection of Jesus, also mentions by name (again, in addition to Mary Magdalene) 'Mary the mother of James and Joseph' but then adds 'the mother of the sons of Zebedee' (Matthew 27:55, 56. See also 27:61; 28:1). John simply speaks of Mary Magdalene.

The variations in those named are no doubt due to the different sources of information available to the Evangelists and their own purposes in writing. Luke, for example, is generally concerned to show us that people of status and influence, as well as the poor and the outcast, responded positively to Jesus – a reason perhaps for specifying Joanna. Matthew seems to have a particular interest in 'the mother of the sons of Zebedee' (that is, James and John), although, intriguingly, she is not named. She appears also in Matthew's account of that significant exchange between Jesus and her sons about the nature of power in God's kingdom (Matthew 20:20-28). Unlike Mark's version, where James and John make the approach to Jesus themselves, in Matthew it is the mother of the sons of Zebedee who takes the initiative in coming to Jesus with an audacious request. She 'came to him with her sons, and kneeling before him, she asked a favour of him.' When Jesus asked what that was, she replied, 'Declare that these two sons of mine will sit, one at your right hand and one at your left, in your kingdom' (20: 20, 21).

In Matthew's Gospel narrative, this episode is set in the midst of Jesus' teaching about the true character of God's kingdom, as he and his followers draw near to Jerusalem and the climax of his crucifixion. It immediately follows one of Jesus' brutally frank Passion predictions (20:17-19). Neither the mother nor her sons, it seems, have cottoned on to Jesus' stark message, let alone his teaching that the kingdom of God is about humility and sacrificial service rather than the exercise of dominant power. They have filtered out the hard bits, leaving a focus on the power and the glory. James and John, after all, are members of Jesus' innermost circle – and Jesus is the Messiah. Surely that means they are entitled to places of power and privilege when Jesus comes into his kingdom.

This pushing for the best places does not go down well with their disciple colleagues – who are all in any case jockeying for position. In what can only be an exercise of godly patience, Jesus tells them all, yet again, that human understandings of power do not apply in God's kingdom:

'It will not be so among you; but whoever wishes to be great among you must be your servant, and whoever wishes to be first among you must be your slave; just as the Son of Man came not to be served but to serve, and to give his life a ransom for many.'

Matthew 20:26-28

We do not know what prompted the mother of the sons of Zebedee to make her approach. Is she, as a mother, seizing an opportunity to promote her sons' cause? She would not be the first or the last mother to do such a thing! Or is she put up to it by her sons, who feel that Jesus might respond more positively to a maternal plea? That phenomenon, too, is not unknown in wider human experience. Whichever it is, the mother (as well as the sons) has let human ambition get the better of her, and so she only hears from Jesus what she wants to hear. In that, she can be for us both a salutary warning and an encouragement – the latter because we see in her a flawed human being like us, who is nonetheless accepted and valued and dealt with patiently by the Lord. And then there she is, watching as he dies on the cross. If she has not learned her lesson already, she is learning by bitter experience now. But there, faithfully, she stays.

That is all we know of her, however. Indeed, a common factor relating to all those referred to is that we are told very little of what we might now call their backstory. We know tantalisingly little about them. But when we reflect on their part in the story of Jesus, they become rather more than mere names on a page. Indeed, even the shadowy 'many' emerge more into the light. We have good reason to be heartily thankful for them. They play a vital role in resourcing the mission of Jesus. Where would that be without them? Though Jesus, it seems, like Joseph is a carpenter (Mark 6:3), there is no indication in the Gospels that he seeks to finance his public ministry by plying his trade. All his focus is on doing the work God has sent him to do. Proclaiming the kingdom of God is his priority. And he seems to have an increasingly strong conviction that his time for this is short.

In making their provision for him, the women play a key part in making possible his single-minded focus. Thank God for them, therefore. Thank God, too, for their bold discipleship, which culminates in their faithful witnessing of Jesus' terrible death and their bearing witness to the truth of his Resurrection. Without them, the Gospel narrative would be a rather different story.

Jesus, too, surely appreciates their support – and not just in material terms. We recall that, to begin with at least, his own family (for their own well-motivated reasons) seek to subvert rather than support his mission. The women who provide him with their committed allegiance, as well as their money, must have become like his new extended family – 'sisters' who risked all to do the will of God (Mark 3:31-35). How that must have encouraged and strengthened him.

Truly, these women deserve to be honoured.

CHAPTER 4

Encounters with unnamed women

We have already shone a spotlight on those women named in the Gospels as members of Jesus' family or among his friends and supporters. Their number is not inconsiderable. But they do not stand alone. According to all the Gospels, Jesus has a surprising number of encounters with women who are not named – surprising because of the generally strict conventions of the time regarding communication between the sexes. Public exchanges were frowned upon. Yet Jesus has no hesitation in responding just as readily to women who approach him as he does to men. Where there is a seeming reluctance (as, for example, in the case of the Syrophoenician woman), it is not to do with gender.

Some of these women are mentioned in our previous reflections – the mother of James and John, the 'many others' who provide for Jesus and his ministry, the woman crying out in the crowd concerning the blessedness of his mother. In this chapter we consider those other unnamed women with whom Jesus has largely one-off encounters as he goes about his mission. We begin by looking at the episodes recorded in Mark's Gospel, most of which have parallels in one or both of Matthew and Luke. We then turn our attention to incidents recorded only by Luke (who seems to have a particular interest in the part women play in the story of Jesus). Finally, we focus on two highly significant encounters between Jesus and unnamed women found only in the Gospel of John.

Simon's mother-in-law
(Mark 1:29-31; Matthew 8:14, 15; Luke 4:38, 39)

Though the accounts of this episode are tantalisingly brief, they do give us some important indicators regarding the way Jesus goes about his ministry, as well as the personal circumstances of his followers. Simon, it seems, is married when he responds to the call of Jesus and leaves his livelihood to become a disciple (Mark 1:16-18). We can only imagine what his wife might have made of this! What we do know, from what Paul says in 1 Corinthians 9:5, is that Peter's wife (*Cephas* is the Aramaic word for Peter) appears to accompany him on his post-Pentecost missionary activities and, by implication, is also a believer. At this later stage, at least, they are together in following Jesus. Perhaps that applies from the outset. Certainly, Jesus seems to use 'the house of Simon and Andrew' (Mark 1:29) as something of a home-base when in Capernaum. That venue is mentioned on a number of occasions. It seems to accommodate an extended household which, when Jesus and his entourage are there, becomes even more extensive!

Leaving everything to do God's work does not, it appears, necessarily involve abandoning family and all home comforts. Jesus benefits from that fact, too. But his teaching makes it clear that the disciple's radical priority, like his, has to be responding to the will of God, wherever that leads.

According to Mark and Luke, the incident involving Simon's mother-in-law takes place on the Sabbath, just after Jesus has performed a startling exorcism in the synagogue. Even at this early stage in their discipleship, 'Simon and Andrew, with James and John' (Mark 1:29) have acquired first-hand experience of the authoritative power of Jesus to bring healing. It is not surprising, therefore, that 'at once'

(Mark 1:30) they tell him of Simon's mother-in-law's predicament. Jesus responds with equal promptness.

She is suffering from an unspecified fever ('a high fever', according to Luke the physician, Luke 4:38). Whatever it is, it is serious enough to incapacitate her. What happens when Jesus arrives is an instantaneous healing. The Evangelists give us varying (but not necessarily contradictory) details as to the way Jesus does it. According to Luke, 'he stood over her and rebuked the fever, and it left her' (Luke 4:39). Here Jesus is still very much in the commanding mode of action so recently displayed in the synagogue – a sign, perhaps, that sickness does not come by the hand of God. According to Mark (whom Matthew follows) Jesus 'came and took her by the hand and lifted her up. Then the fever left her' (Mark 1:31; see also Matthew 8:15).

Mark's mention of touch is significant. In a good many of Jesus' healing acts, he either touches the sufferer or is touched by them. So he identifies with something common and instinctive in our human experience. When something is wrong with us, we invariably touch or hold the area that is troubling us. When we are seeking to express care or sympathy, our first instinct is often to turn to physical contact – a hug, the touch of a hand. Those involved in medicine use touch a good deal in the course of diagnosis and treatment. In the context of our health and well-being, body language plays a vital part. Jesus is clearly well aware of this.

In relation to Simon's mother-in-law, Mark alone gives us the detail that Jesus not only touches her hand but holds it, and in so doing 'lifted her up'. He helps her to her feet. That action is so typical of the caring Jesus.

The one restored to health responds in a way that is no doubt typical of *her*. She straightaway gets on with supplying

Jesus and the others with a meal. As Jesus has ministered to her need, so now she ministers to his – with body language of her own.

Jairus' daughter
(Mark 5:21-43; Matthew 9:18-26; Luke 8:40-56)

The raising of Jairus' daughter from death is closely associated with the dramatic healing of another female character, the woman with a seemingly unstoppable issue of blood. The two events are sandwiched together, with the child's situation forming the outside sections and the woman's coming in the middle. Both speak of how Jesus responds to desperation, bringing new life and hope.

First we encounter the child's father, Jairus, suddenly faced with the awful prospect of the death of his beloved (unnamed) daughter. Faced with this, considerations of reputation and dignity become as nothing for this respected leader of the synagogue. Though he must know that his religious colleagues and teachers regard Jesus with great suspicion, he risks his good standing with them by publicly throwing himself at Jesus' feet. Here, he desperately wants to believe, is someone who *can* help him. That is all that matters. So, in front of a great crowd of witnesses, he abases himself and repeatedly begs Jesus to do something. Who cares what anyone else thinks. This is raw need, and he knows where to go with it.

It is to Mark's account that we must look for the most vivid depiction of this crisis. Mark the Evangelist is a master storyteller, and he knows the importance of lively narrative and apparently incidental detail. Matthew, on the other hand, is fairly ruthless in his editing, here and in other material he shares with Mark, leaving only what he considers to be the essential facts of the matter. Luke, though a little more fulsome in his account of this episode, is also more restrained than Mark.

According to Mark, Jairus pleads with Jesus ('repeatedly') in these words: 'My little daughter is at the point of death. Come and lay your hands on her, so that she may be made well, and live' (Mark 5:23). We notice that, although (as we learn later) the child is 12 years old and therefore in that culture on the verge of adulthood, her father uses a diminutive word to refer to her – 'my *little* daughter'. How eloquent this is of the way she is regarded by her father. It is a term of great affection. This girl-child is clearly much loved and cherished. Luke gives us the added detail that she is an only daughter, and no doubt all the more precious for that. Losing her would be devastating.

Jairus evidently already has faith in the power of Jesus to heal. It is not just desperation speaking. He knows Jesus' track record in this regard and believes that if only Jesus will come and do something, all will be well. That 'something', we note, is to lay his hands on the child – to exercise again, as he has done for others, the healing power of touch.

And how does Jesus respond to Jairus' heartfelt pleas? Mark's typical one-liner says it all: 'So he went with him' (Mark 5:24). No ifs or buts and no further interrogation. However, though that joint journey ultimately issues in Jairus' daughter being restored to him, it turns out that some undesired waiting is required. No doubt to Jairus' great consternation (and the testing of his faith), Jesus delays in order to address the needs of another in desperate need. We shall look at her situation in the next section.

While Jesus is dealing with this interruption (though this is not how Jesus sees it), the news comes that Jairus has been dreading. His daughter has died. He has not managed to get Jesus there in time. All is lost.

But not so. Jesus overhears what has been said and immediately says to Jairus, 'Do not fear, only believe' (Mark 5:36). A tall order – though looking at Jesus as he speaks these words may help Jairus to hold on to hope. This is someone who seems to speak with holy authority, and whose very presence backs that up. So they continue on to Jairus' home. At this stage, Jesus allows only his most trusted disciples – Peter, James and John – to accompany him. All the focus now has to be on bringing the child back to life, without the distraction of noisy crowds. As well as aiding Jesus in his ministry, this shows his sensitivity to the best interests of a vulnerable young girl. She needs her family but not hordes of gawping onlookers.

So those causing a tumult and weeping and wailing loudly (no doubt including professional mourners, who would normally attend such events) are summarily banished from the scene – but not before they laugh at him for saying the child is not dead but sleeping. What exactly he means by that is a debatable point. Does he perceive that the girl is not actually dead but unconscious, or is the metaphor of sleeping a way of describing death which suggests that this is not to be the final outcome (a manner of speech he also employs in the case of Lazarus – see John 11)? Whichever it is, those mourners already present certainly take him to mean that the child is still alive, and that notion to them is laughable. They know death when they see it.

What happens next is an intimate scene of healing and restoration. The only people now present are Jairus' daughter and her parents, with Jesus, Peter, James and John. Again we see Jesus using body language. He takes the prone child by the hand. Then he speaks to her, using Aramaic, then the common language of the people. Happily Mark has preserved his words for us, as well as supplying a translation: "'*Talitha cum*", which means, "Little girl, get up!"' (Mark 5:41). We notice that Jesus follows her father's example in using a diminutive term of affection. That is indicative of what must have been his tone of voice. He is speaking to her in a way she can understand and with a caring voice which reaches into her depths, encouraging her to respond. She does so 'immediately', says Mark, using one of his favourite words, and begins to walk around. To say that her parents are 'overcome with amazement' (Mark 5:42) must be something of an understatement! How thankful Jairus must be that he went out on a limb and approached Jesus.

It is Jesus who points out their daughter's next, immediate need – something to eat, to help restore her strength. Jesus is nothing if not holistic in his approach to human well-being. He also 'strictly ordered' those present (note the change of tone) not to blaze this wonder abroad. It is not the only time that Jesus gives such an order (especially in Mark's Gospel). He is very concerned not to be categorised as a wonder-worker. That is not his primary mission. He has come to proclaim the kingdom of God. His healing acts of power are signs of that kingdom, signs that God wills the health of all creation. They point to a God of love. But the love of God also brings radical challenge – the call to repentance and a way of life fully committed to God's values. Marvelling at amazing things is no substitute for that.

There is no record of Jesus conversing with the 'little girl' after she was raised from her deathbed, but it seems highly unlikely that he would ignore her! What memories she must have carried forward into her subsequent life. And despite Jesus' strictures, what a tale she must have told. How good it would be to know what became of her.

The woman with an issue of blood

On the way to Jairus' house, Jesus has a significant encounter with another unnamed woman in distress.

This woman's trauma has gone on for years. Not only is her condition personally difficult and debilitating, it also renders her, in ritual terms, permanently 'unclean', and therefore relegated to the fringes of her own community. How appropriate, therefore, that her restoration comes through touching the fringes of the Lord's clothing. The merest and most lowly of contacts is enough. And the result is immediate.

Unlike Jairus, the woman approaches Jesus secretly. She is taking quite a risk – risking a man's wrath because her touching him will make him also ritually unclean. And there is no guarantee that it will work. Indeed, at first, despite the fact that her longing has at last been fulfilled, it seems that there will be some punishing consequences. 'Jesus turned about in the crowd and said, "Who touched my clothes?" . . . He looked all round to see who had done it.' No wonder she falls down before him 'in fear and trembling' (Mark 5:30-33). Yet, as ever, the Lord's intention is to raise up, not to cast down. The woman, so long rejected, hears herself addressed as 'Daughter'. Her risk of faith, even though she has tried to keep it hidden, has been more than justified. Not only has she been healed – that alone would be cause enough for rejoicing – but she has also been raised to her feet, both literally and metaphorically, by the one who has healed her, that Lord who addresses her not with condemnation or condescension but with an intimate term of belonging: 'Daughter, your faith has made you well; go in peace, and be healed of your disease' (Mark 5:34). She *matters* to Jesus. That makes all the difference in the world. It is more than her disease that has been attended to.

The Syrophoenician/Canaanite woman
(Matthew 15:21-28; Mark 7:24-30)

Both Matthew and Mark offer us an account of an encounter between Jesus and an unnamed Gentile woman, on Gentile territory. For once, Matthew gives us the most detailed and graphic version, but both present us with an episode that is notoriously difficult to interpret. Perhaps focusing on the woman involved might give us a helpful perspective.

Her encounter with Jesus is highly charged and one in which the language of love seems at first to be set in a harsh key. We recall, for example, that at that time, for both Jews and Greeks, the word 'dog' was frequently used as a term of contempt. But surface appearances are not always the true story.

So let us look at this woman: like so many, defined not by her name but by race and background – 'a Gentile, of Syrophoenician origin,' says Mark; 'a Canaanite woman,' says Matthew. Whatever her precise origin might have been, she has been neatly categorised – labelled – opening the way to all manner of assumptions and abuses.

A Gentile – a pagan – an outsider – a woman. Prime candidate for exclusion, dismissal and treatment with contempt.

Look at this woman: throwing herself at the feet of Jesus and begging. Like so many before and since, she is taking the risk of being rejected, humiliated, quite literally kicked out of the way – and risking all this in order to get to the resources she needs to help her child. Here is a woman of courage and determination – she is willing to demean herself, to endure anything so that her child might be saved. She acts alone, without support or protection. Sadly, even in our day and age, she is not unique.

In the culture of her time, she should not do what she does. But she is careless of convention and prohibition. Her care for her daughter overcomes all else. What are ritual taboos, what are racial and religious prejudices in the face of crying human need?

This Jew with a reputation has travelled into Gentile territory. He has taken a risk. He has laid himself open. If he has gone that far, there is just the possibility that he might be willing to cross further boundaries. The opportunity is there. She will seize it – whatever the consequences.

Look at this woman, grovelling on the ground – and listen to the dialogue that ensues. Like so many others before and since, here is a woman of spirit, initiative, tenacity and wit. Her true place is not on the floor.

Despite the entreaties of his disciples to get rid of her, and his own initial refusal to engage with her ('But he did not answer her at all,' as Matthew baldly puts it), Jesus now enters into conversation with her. That in itself shatters convention. This conversation gives her the chance to show who she really is – a woman of worth, a woman who can hold her head high.

The dialogue between the woman and Jesus is a fascinating one, open to much speculation. Why is the response of Jesus apparently so harsh? Is he annoyed by her interruption? That would be a very human reaction for one facing exhaustion in ministry. He has, after all, according to Mark, come for some peace and quiet. Is he asserting the primacy of God's chosen people (the children come first) and the chosen focus of his mission agenda? That does not sit easily with his general willingness to consort with Gentiles (see, for example, Matthew 8:5-13; 8:28-34) and his strong emphasis on God's care for the outsider (see, for example, Luke 4:16-30, which is, in effect, his radical mission statement). Is he testing the woman's faith? Does he even have something to learn from her? Does she act as an irritant, provoking in him a deeper awareness of his true vocation (rather like the mother of Jesus at the outset of John's Gospel)? Or, discerning her character, is Jesus giving her back her dignity; lifting her to her feet, metaphorically if not actually, by provoking into expression her strong sense of justice and agility of mind? Perhaps it is something of all of these. Certainly the woman is in no way shamed, and she gets what she wants.

Indeed, more. Typically of Jesus, he not only heals the woman's daughter; he also gives back to the woman herself the precious gift of self-respect: 'Woman, great is your faith! Let it be done for you as you wish' (Matthew 15:28).

We should thank God for this unnamed woman, and many like her over the centuries. They are signs of God's kingdom.

The widow and her offering (Mark 12:41-44; Luke 21:1-4)

This incident occurs as Jesus approaches the climax of his ministry, which will result in his brutal death. In Mark's account, it follows a series of forthright verbal clashes in the Jerusalem Temple precincts with religious authorities and official teachers. Jesus has just warned those around him to beware of them, for they 'like to walk around in long robes, and to be greeted with respect in the market-places, and to have the best seats in the synagogues and places of honour at banquets!' 'They devour widows' houses,' he went on to say, 'and for the sake of appearance say long prayers.' 'They will receive the greater condemnation,' is his verdict on them (Mark 12:38-40). Hypocrisy, self-interest and exploitation of the vulnerable are his charges. Such traits are by no means confined to first-century Jerusalem.

Jesus' message is brought home by the appearance of a real-life visual aid – a widow who, from her poverty, makes an extravagant offering for the work of the Temple. Extravagant, that is, in terms of the limits of her resources, not the actual amount. What she put into the collection box is the smallest of small change to those of greater wealth. For her, that offering probably deprives her of at least her next meal. It comes from the sacrificial devotion of her heart. She does not do it for show. And as with the anonymous woman who is shortly to anoint him, Jesus commends her for the abundance of her love. Hers is not an ostentatious gesture. In terms of giving, it is the real thing.

The collection boxes of the Temple treasury were located in the Court of the Women – that area of the Temple which was the furthest women could go without trespassing on the more sacred parts of the building. They were regarded as unfit to tread the holy courts. Yet the Holy One of God, sitting also on the margins, proclaims not only this widow's worth but also her significance as an example of true religion (see James 1:27).

And she probably has no idea that she is being commended in this way. Seeking no recognition, she simply and quietly does what she can – and more. Her reward is surely great in heaven.

The anointing woman of Mark 14
(Mark 14:1-11; Matthew 26:6-13)

'Truly I tell you,' says the Markan Jesus, 'wherever the good news is proclaimed in the whole world, what she has done will be told in remembrance of her' (Mark 14:9).

'In remembrance of her.' We know not who she is or why she does what she does. This anonymous woman bursts onto the scene and then disappears again. She risks her whole reputation to gatecrash a gathering of men and indulge in highly charged and extravagant body language. Sheer foolishness. But it strikes a deep chord with one who expresses the foolishness of God.

This woman from the edge anoints Jesus on the edge of his Passion.

It is worth meditating a little further on this dramatic incident. We might even find that it somehow connects with our story – that it breaks through the boundaries of culture and time – that 'remembering' it discloses a vividly present reality.

It is certainly not there in Mark's narrative by accident. Thank God we are now recognising that Mark the Evangelist is not only a master storyteller; he is also a telling theologian. He chooses his material carefully. There is a point to its inclusion, and its context.

By the beginning of chapter 14, Mark has his audience on the edge of their seats. His narrative has become increasingly tense, increasingly terse and increasingly stark. Passion has begun in earnest. And of all the Evangelists, Mark gives us the bleakest picture of crucifixion.

Into the gathering darkness comes an unnamed woman with a jar of very costly ointment. Her act of anointing is poignant in the extreme. Mark relates it in one of his favourite literary forms – the sandwich. Here the outer slices of the sandwich are very bitter – their 'flavours' are conspiracy and betrayal: conspiracy on the part of the religious authorities, 'the chief priests and the scribes', the ones who should be the first to recognise God's moment when it comes. Their opposition is not unheralded. From the early days of his ministry, Jesus has clashed with those forces and attitudes that stand against his proclamation of God's kingdom – with pride and jealousy, with the increasingly desperate defence of vested interests and power structures, with narrow definitions and blind hypocrisy. It is interesting that whichever strand of Gospel material we look at, those negative forces cluster around the ones in spiritual leadership, the guardians of holy tradition. Such guardians bring Jesus to a vicious death. It is one of the greatest of tragic ironies (and one poignantly highlighted by Mark) that, in the name of religious purity, religious experts condemn as blasphemous the one who is religion's fulfilment. It seems that trained theologians can find Jesus very hard to take.

Conspiring by the leadership; betrayal by 'one of the twelve' (Mark 14:10) – one of that motley crew of men called out by Jesus to be the agents of a renewed Israel. Of all the Evangelists, Mark makes us most graphically aware of their persistent incomprehension and failure. Judas is an extreme case – but he by no means stands alone.

Between this sorry tale of male-dominated power politics and knife-in-the-back loyalty is sandwiched something beautiful, something profoundly meaningful, something that flies in the face of convention, something that is balm to Christ's troubled soul: the reckless act of a devoted woman. Notice that in Mark's account (followed by Matthew) she is not labelled stereotypically as 'sinner woman'. No comment is passed on her morals. But as a woman, she is one of those low-status folk who again and again seem to get near to the heart of things.

We might note in passing that the narrative is set in the house of Simon the leper. Presumably if Simon is living in Bethany he has been given official clearance from the skin disease that afflicted him (then regarded as 'unclean' and requiring isolation from the community). But labels stick, like mud. Yet Jesus has no inhibitions about associating with lepers, cured or otherwise. Where the outcast is, there is Jesus also.

For some unspecified reason, the woman comes uninvited to the dinner, breaks open a jar of very costly ointment and pours the contents on the head of Jesus. Her act of devotion is costly in a material as well as in a personal sense. The jar of ointment is worth the equivalent of a year's wages. Hence the complaints of prodigal waste by the rather more hard-headed supper guests. But Jesus, the self-expression of an extravagant God, accepts and publicly affirms both the extravagant gesture and its perpetrator: 'Let her alone', he says. 'Let her alone . . . She has done a beautiful thing to me' (Mark 14:6, RSV).

What the complainants fail to perceive is a deeper truth. At Passover, the custom is to give to the poor. What they cannot see is that in front of them is the very epitome of poverty. The Markan Jesus has become increasingly isolated, even from his close followers, misunderstood, conspired against, ridiculed and rejected. He is being inescapably stripped of all that makes life good. He ends up, in total poverty, on the cross – stripped physically, emotionally and spiritually.

Here in Bethany, what a tremendous gift this woman's action and attitude must be to him. She loves him and she shows it, never mind what others think of her. She provides something of that understanding and tender loving care he must long for in the midst of so much hateful opposition. And she does it without speaking a word. What a difference a generous gesture of love can make when all around have their knives out.

'She has done what she could,' affirms Jesus (Mark 14:8). What an epitaph. As a woman, few avenues are open to her, but that does not stop her taking action. She does what she can – and with no apology. And her wordless gesture opens up truth in ways that can scarcely be imagined. She is anticipating the death of Jesus – and its untimely nature. She is also performing a highly significant theological act. According to Mark, she anoints Christ's head. Such anointings are appropriate to kings and are normally carried out by recognised religious authorities, especially priests. By extension, the longed-for messianic descendant of King David would be the Christ, 'the Anointed One'. The implications of this are little short of shocking. This unnamed woman, denied any public function in the religion of her day, in fact performs a momentous, not to say priestly, function. She anoints the Christ.

It is fitting, perhaps, that an unrecognised woman with no rights should anoint the unrecognised Messiah, about to be hounded to death by the official representatives of God. Mark knew a thing or two.

This messianic anointing is a preparation for burial. Yet in the paradoxical love of God, it is an integral part of the good news. For the burial of Christ will lead to the bursting out of the unconquerable life of God, to the glorious Easter message that not even all the massed forces of evil can destroy love, forgiveness and hope.

And he who on Maundy Thursday tells his followers to eat bread and drink wine in remembrance of him also says that this other Holy Week event will be told in remembrance of her. How fitting that seems.

The anointing 'sinner woman' in Luke (Luke 7:36-50)

Luke offers us another anointing episode, this time involving a different woman and at a different stage in Jesus' ministry.

It occurs at a relatively early point in his public mission, in the house of Simon the Pharisee. He has been invited there for a meal, no doubt to be given the 'once-over' by a cautious officialdom. He has been causing quite a stir and not exactly showing proper respect for the religious authorities. It would not be surprising if Simon wants to take a closer look at him, to check him out.

Whatever his motive in inviting him, Simon has evidently omitted to ensure that his guest receives the usual welcoming niceties – a kiss of greeting, the washing of feet to freshen up (very needful in a hot and dusty sandal-wearing environment), and the anointing of the head to signify gladness at the arrival of the visitor.

Though he has failed to observe the conventions of hospitality, Simon the Pharisee is nonetheless a respectable religious leader, committed to righteous behaviour. So he is shocked when his fascinating guest allows an uninvited intruder – 'a woman in the city, who was a sinner' (a euphemism for a prostitute) – to subject him to some extravagant and decidedly sensuous body language. Simon says to himself, 'If this man were a prophet, he would have known who and what kind of woman this is who is touching him' (Luke 7:39). She obviously has a reputation. And Jesus clearly has some questions to answer.

The response of Jesus is a lesson in divine love. After telling Simon a very pointed parable about the effects of forgiveness, he says to him:

> 'Do you see this woman? I entered your house; you gave me no water for my feet, but she has bathed my feet with her tears and dried them with her hair. You gave me no kiss, but from the time I came in she has not stopped kissing my feet. You did not anoint my head with oil,

but she has anointed my feet with ointment. Therefore, I tell you, her sins, which were many, have been forgiven; hence she has shown great love. But the one to whom little is forgiven, loves little.'

Luke 7:44-47

Luke gives us a significant little detail here. Before Jesus speaks the words just quoted, we are told that he turns towards the woman (as was the custom, the guests would be reclining around the table, so the woman behind Jesus would have had ready access to his feet, and he could quite naturally have turned his gaze upon her). Jesus speaks words of rebuke to Simon while looking at the woman whose actions he is affirming. She would know from his face, his words and his tone of voice that he appreciates her reckless gesture and understands where it is coming from – not from sin or seduction but from love born of overwhelming gratitude for the experience of loving forgiveness. He does not just tolerate what she is doing; he does not just allow her to do it. Rather, he is grateful to her for her ministry. The gratitude works both ways – one based on the enormity of forgiveness, the other on a very human need for tender, loving care.

No doubt this unnamed woman has not encountered a man like Jesus before – a man whose evident love and valuing of her does not involve the purchase of her bodily favours or the exploitation of her vulnerability. And there is more. This man has a strangely perceptive authority which penetrates the heart of her condition. He sees her sin, certainly. There is no question of that. But he also sees *her*. He sees the *whole* truth about her. And he sees her faith, embryonic though it might be, as she responds to his care in the only way she knows how – with expressive body language.

This woman takes on board the reality of God's forgiveness, mediated through Jesus, and surely also senses her potential to lead a different kind of life. The truth of love has set her free, causing the true love latent within her to well up from the depths. Truly, the kingdom of God is open to her (see Matthew 21:31).

Does Simon learn this lesson of love? We do not know. Nor do we know what becomes of this anointing woman. What we do see in this episode, however, is the truth and power of that divine reality succinctly expressed in 1 Peter 4:8: 'Love covers a multitude of sins.' In God's mercy, it still does.

The woman bent double *(Luke 13:10-17)*

> She stood up straight and began praising God.
>
> *Luke 13:13*

What an encounter. What a transformation. On this Sabbath day, in this place of worship, this woman is liberated – set free from that gross distortion of obeisance into which she has been locked for 18 long years. Because of the initiative and the action of Jesus, she can express her undoubtedly heartfelt praises standing up straight, looking her Saviour in the eye, face to face with the one who has raised her up. In this place of prayer, she becomes a living paradigm of true worship. What a cause for rejoicing.

Yet what is this? The leader of this house of prayer is clearly not best pleased. The rules have been broken – sacred rules. He does not have the gall to confront Jesus directly, so he berates the congregation and, not least, by implication the woman herself. If you want to be healed, follow the proper process. Come on the right day. It is an attitude recognisable in many contexts, secular as well as religious.

But it provokes from Jesus a robust and revealing response. In no uncertain terms, he faces the leadership with the inconsistency, not to say hypocrisy, of their stance. As Luke relates, Jesus puts the opposition to shame by pointing up the priorities of *God*. Yes, after all this time the woman could have waited one more day for her healing – her life was not in immediate danger. According to the rules, had it been, then action on the Sabbath would have been justified. But the rule of God – the *kingdom* of God – is not about observing or interpreting regulations. It is about working for the well-being of all creation, and doing whatever is necessary, at all times and in all places, to fulfil that end. Even on the Sabbath. Indeed, that is what the Sabbath is about. That is what *God* is about. The woman presents with her evident need. She says not a word, but her very condition is her unspoken prayer and says it all. She is thirsting for help just as much as any tethered ox or donkey, and the embodiment of God's kingly rule is not about to ignore her. He responds, even without a specific verbal request.

And Jesus does not then mince his words with the leader of the synagogue and the other murmurers. 'You hypocrites!' he says, in decidedly undiplomatic language, 'Does not each of you on the sabbath untie his ox or his donkey from the manger, and lead it away to give it water? And ought not this woman, a daughter of Abraham whom Satan bound for eighteen long years, be set free from this bondage on the sabbath day?' (Luke 13: 15, 16).

'A daughter of Abraham.' This is the only place in all the canonical Scriptures where that phrase occurs, and it is redolent with meaning. It says, more than anything else, that this woman *belongs* – belongs to the community of faith, belongs to God's chosen people, belongs to *God!* This in itself must rejoice her heart. A woman with a disability at that time was likely to be doubly handicapped. Female, therefore only acceptable on certain, restrictive terms. Disabled, therefore no doubt she and/or her family must have sinned.

Not so, not so, says Jesus. She is a daughter of Abraham. She belongs. She can stand up straight. She can worship. She can know that God values her enough to take the initiative, to reach out and touch her, to set her free, to bring her to her full stature. She can know that she is worth far more to God than apparent religious rectitude and the approval of the powers that be.

In Luke's Gospel, this is the last recorded instance of Jesus being in a synagogue. His visits to these community places of worship are rarely, it seems, characterised by peaceful calm. On the contrary, and – it has to be said – largely because of the provocation of Jesus himself, they tend to be occasions of conflict and dramatic encounter. The first episode both sets the tone and indicates the reason for it. His teaching at the synagogue in Nazareth (Luke 4:16-30) nearly sees him hurled off a cliff and killed. From being 'amazed at the gracious words that came from his mouth', his home congregation become enraged at him when he goes on to point out that God's gracious activity extends beyond the defined boundaries of the chosen people. It is here that Jesus sets out his agenda, using the words of Isaiah:

'The Spirit of the Lord is upon me,
because he has anointed me
to bring good news to the poor.
He has sent me to proclaim release to the captives
and recovery of sight to the blind,
to let the oppressed go free,
to proclaim the year of the Lord's favour.'
Luke 4:18, 19, quoting Isaiah 61:1, 2

Jesus has no hesitation in putting this agenda into action, whatever the consequences and whatever the context, Sabbath days in the synagogues very much included. The healing of the woman bent double should be seen clearly in this light. The long-term captive is released, the oppressed one is set free. The Lord's favour rules over all.

Why then, again and again, does it provoke such resistance and hostility – as it still does today? The rule of God – that 'kingdom that cannot be shaken', to use the terminology of Hebrews (12:28) – still has the potential (and the potency) to clash with our established ways. We are safe and secure within our own frameworks of rules and practices, hallowed by the use of many years. All well and good. Jesus himself can hardly be faulted on his rigorous spiritual discipline. But that discipline serves only to keep him focused on the presence and the prompting of God. It is not an end in itself. That way lies idolatry.

Making God in the image of our hallowed rules is not only unwise; it is also disabling, stultifying and oppressive. It bows us down. It is a shutting of the door on grace. Accepting the values and the ground rules of the kingdom of God, on the other hand, though it might shake us to the core, leaves us standing up straight, full of God's praises and, with the Spirit's empowering, ready at all times to raise others to their full stature in the purpose of God.

The encounter between Jesus and the woman bent double thus faces us with challenge, as well as rejoicing. And it highlights another crucial message. Using the language of his day, Jesus says that Satan bound this woman for 18 long years. Whatever we make of this imagery, the message behind it is clear. Disability is not a visitation by God. In every sense of the phrase, God wants us to stand up straight. In many and various ways, and in a creation given its freedom, God ever works towards that end.

The widow of Nain *(Luke 7:11-17)*

Concern and compassion for widows are characteristics of God (see, for example, Deuteronomy 10:18; Psalm 68:5), characteristics which God expects and requires will be shared by the community of faith. That much is clear from the Scriptures, both Jewish and Christian. On not a few occasions, provision for widows is cited as a sign and a test of appropriate behaviour for God's people (see, for example, Deuteronomy 27:19; James 1:27).

Being bereaved of a partner is hard in any age or culture. When the experience is compounded by practical need, that hardship becomes even more acute. In the context Luke is describing, there is no welfare state. Widows with no independent means are very much dependent on what family they have and the goodwill of those among whom they live. Daily life can be precarious. They need support.

From the strictures found throughout the Scriptural texts, it is evident that such support was not always forthcoming: indeed, abusive treatment and exploitation were far from unknown. God's expectations were by no means always met. Even the earliest Jerusalem Church, in the first flush of its enthusiasm, had a notorious falling-out over the way widows were treated (Acts 6:1). On all sorts of levels, not least dealing with practical needs and being at the mercy of the attitudes and behaviour of others with power, widowhood was a challenging experience.

Jesus is well aware of this. He is publicly very critical of those who mistreat widows and should know better (see especially Mark 12:40; Luke 20:47). As we shall see later (see chapter 5), one of his most telling parables has to do with an ill-treated widow and her feisty response. It is not surprising, then, that when he encounters a widow burying her only son, he takes the initiative and comes to her aid in a most dramatic way. As in other situations where crying need presents itself to him, Jesus does not wait for any formal request to do something. He simply gets on with addressing the need – on this occasion, one suspects, to the great surprise of the widow concerned. She has not sought Jesus out. In human terms, this encounter was an 'accidental' one.

In relating this episode, Luke uses language which brings to mind the restoration of another son to his mother, centuries earlier (1 Kings 17:8-24). Under God's direction, the great prophet Elijah had billeted himself with a widow in Zarephath (in Sidon) at a time of severe drought and famine. She had a son. As Elijah had promised, the three of them were provided for in their need. But then the son died, stirring up in the widow both distress and anger. Accompanied by a prayer remonstrating with God, Elijah takes action, bringing breath back into the boy's body. Then, we are told, Elijah took the child and 'gave him to his mother' (1 Kings 17:23). That same phrase is used by Luke of Jesus restoring her son to the widow of Nain. The crowds milling around outside Nain's city gate evidently caught the association, saying, 'A great prophet has risen among us!' (Luke 7:15, 16).

Jesus himself has already made reference to the widow of Zarephath. He brought opprobrium on himself when in the synagogue at Nazareth he pointed out that 'there were many widows in Israel at the time of Elijah . . . yet Elijah was sent to none of them except to a widow at Zarephath in Sidon' (Luke 4:25, 26). That did not go down well. The woman of Nain, however, is a widow in Israel, albeit in the border regions of southern Galilee. Jesus responds to need where and when it is presented to him.

Here his response arises out of his compassion for the widow, who in losing her only son is likely to suffer more than emotional hardship. Jesus, one way or another, has clearly sussed out the situation. We learn from his words to the corpse that the son concerned was a young man and therefore might have been expected to provide many years of support to his mother. Her loss was grievous indeed. Knowing this, Jesus speaks to her first. We may imagine his encouraging and understanding tone of voice as he says to her, 'Do not weep' (Luke 7:13). He wants her to feel, first and foremost, that he cares – but he also wants to convey that he will do something to help, something that will banish her mourning.

He then touches the bier, as a sign to the bearers to stop. By doing so, he renders himself ritually unclean, but this matters not to Jesus. He addresses the body: 'Young man, I say to you, rise!' (Luke 7:14). To everyone's fear and amazement, no doubt not least his mother's, 'the dead man sat up and began to speak'. Jesus then 'gave him to his mother' (Luke 7:15). He brings them together again, thus meeting the widow's need and affording both mother and son a new lease of life. The widow's response is not recorded for us, but how heartfelt it must be – probably a whole mixture of overwhelming emotions. Her gratitude must be immense. Not that Jesus asks for that. Compassion has done its work, and Jesus simply goes on his way.

The 'daughters of Jerusalem' (Luke 23:27-31)

The context for this encounter is near the climax of Jesus' mission, as he is led out of Jerusalem to be crucified. As he was arrested in Gethsemane garden the night before, he said to those who took him, 'this is your hour, and the power of darkness!' (Luke 22:53). But, after struggling in prayer, he had willingly given himself over to this dark hour, trusting that from it his Father in heaven was going to bring a great salvation – not just for him but for the whole world. As the well-known hymn puts it, 'We may not know, we cannot tell, what pains he had to bear'.[2] Quite literally, Jesus goes through hell. And all for love – the absolute, indestructible love of God for the whole of wayward creation.

Now Jesus is being taken out to suffer this tortuous death. Crucifixion is not a quick or a 'clean' means of execution. Already the cost is apparent. A bystander (Simon of Cyrene) has to be drafted in to carry the cross, the implication being that after what has happened so far, Jesus is too physically weakened to manage this heavy load (Luke 23:26). A significant crowd is accompanying this progress to Calvary. That is how the Roman occupiers of the land want it to be. The one to be executed has to be disgraced as publicly as possible, not least to act as a deterrent to those under occupation.

This crowd no doubt includes those who shortly before, in exchanges with Pontius Pilate, were baying for blood. As Luke puts it, 'they kept urgently demanding with loud shouts that he should be crucified'. And in a telling description of Pilate's capitulation to mob rule, Luke goes on, 'and their voices prevailed' (Luke 23:23). Yet by the time Jesus dies,

---

2. 'There is a green hill far away', Cecil Frances Alexander (1818–1895).

the crowd's tone seems to have changed. Having got what they clamoured for, Luke tells us that 'when all the crowds who had gathered there for this spectacle saw what had taken place, they returned home, beating their breasts' (Luke 23:48). Even the Roman centurion at the scene has by that stage declared Jesus 'innocent' (Luke 23:47).

And among this volatile and changeable crowd are the women whom Jesus addresses as 'daughters of Jerusalem'. Interestingly, the only other place in Scripture where we find this term is in the Song of Songs, that great and sensuous love song in the Jewish tradition. We can only guess why this phrase comes to Jesus' mind at this critical time, but it would perhaps not be surprising if the Lord of love has an affinity with this highly charged text. Certainly, the Christian Church has subsequently interpreted the Song of Songs in terms of the divine Lover and his people.

Here, however, the tone is much more fraught and taut. Love is being tested to the limit. Yet despite the message he has for these women, Jesus can still speak to them as *daughters* of Jerusalem. He engages with them personally, genuinely concerned for them and their children even in the midst of his own final crisis. They have come, as is their wont, to weep and wail for a condemned man, believing this to be a religious service they can perform (rather like the professional mourners at more natural deaths). But Jesus tells them to weep for themselves and for their children, not for him.

It is clear that before this he has had a growing conviction that Jerusalem is headed for disaster and that its rejection of his mission is making that inevitable. That conviction causes him deep distress. Indeed, it makes *him* weep. Luke tells us that only a few days earlier, as Jesus 'came near and saw the city, he wept over it', bewailing the prospect of its falling to its enemies because it did not recognise the peace he came to bring (Luke 19:41-44; see also 21:20-24). How personally he feels for the holy city comes through in words he uttered while still en route there: 'Jerusalem, Jerusalem, the city that kills the prophets and stones those who are sent to it! How often have I desired to gather your children together as a hen gathers her brood under her wings, and you were not willing!' (Luke 13:34).

That profound, not to say maternal concern, that frustrated longing, is what informs the exchange of Jesus with the daughters of Jerusalem. He feels for them, discerning what will befall them. And he uses imagery that will directly connect with them as women: 'For the days are surely coming when they will say, "Blessed are the barren, and the wombs that never bore, and the breasts that never nursed"' (Luke 23:29). Such women will not have to face the awful prospect of witnessing the destruction of their children. Jesus goes on to quote Hosea 10:8, a text which graphically depicts the desperation of those subjected to attack by a ruthless enemy.

And in AD 70, Jerusalem was indeed brutally subdued by the Romans for rising in rebellion. Many daughters of Jerusalem then had cause to weep bitterly.

Encounters in John's Gospel

John's approach to the story of Jesus is somewhat different to the narratives of Matthew, Mark and Luke. We might describe the Synoptic accounts as 'episodic' – that is, they relate, quite briefly, a whole series of episodes portraying the mission of Jesus from Galilee to Jerusalem. John the Evangelist, on the other hand, tells us of fewer events but goes into greater depth concerning those he selects. Thus we find in his work a series of encounters between Jesus and others which are explored at some length and are intended to point us to the true significance of Jesus and his mission from God. These culminate in the last discourses of Jesus with his disciples on the night before he died, exchanges bristling with meaning which cover the whole of chapters 13–17.

Many of the meaningful and substantial encounters recorded in John's Gospel involve individuals, and not a few of those are women. We have already reflected on those who are 'named' – the mother of Jesus, Martha and Mary, and Mary Magdalene. Two remain who are given no name – a Samaritan woman and a woman caught in the act of adultery. We turn now to look at these two controversial women and how Jesus engages with them.

The woman of Samaria (John 4:1-42)

What a fascinating woman this is – and one who clearly gives an exhausted Jesus fresh energy to carry out his mission of reaping the harvest of God, whenever and wherever (see verses 31-38).

Jesus, with his disciples, is en route from Judea back to home ground in Galilee. His journey takes him through the land of Samaria. No self-respecting Jew would tarry long in this area. Jews and Samaritans, so to speak, have history. Centuries before, this territory constituted the northern kingdom of Israel. In the eighth century BC, this kingdom was decisively conquered by the great regional power of Assyria. Many of its inhabitants were deported, and people from other areas under Assyria's sway were settled in the land.

Its ethnicity, therefore, became decidedly mixed, as did its religion. So, on both these counts, Samaritans came to be regarded as unacceptable in terms of Jewish heritage and faith. Contact with them, particularly in relation to things like sharing drinking vessels (see verse 9), would render the observant Jew unclean.

It is shocking, therefore, that Jesus initiates and prolongs such contact, and the shock is compounded by the fact that this Samaritan is also a woman. It was not the done thing to talk to a lone woman in this way. No wonder his disciples are 'astonished' (verse 27) when they return from buying food to discover what is going on (though, interestingly, none of them dares question Jesus about it).

At the end of chapter 2, John has shared his conviction that Jesus 'knew all people and needed no one to testify about anyone; for he himself knew what was in everyone' (2:24, 25). That certainly becomes apparent in his encounter with the Samaritan woman. He discerns very quickly, it seems, that here is someone open to an engagement about the truth of God, and he wastes no time in seizing that opportunity. Gender and background matter not. He senses that the woman is ready for an in-depth conversation, and he goes for it. He sees into her soul as well as her personal life.

It soon becomes evident that this woman is indeed ripe for the occasion. She is clearly quick-witted and intelligent, as well as knowledgeable about religious matters. She is also in a less than regular personal relationship, and the fact that she has come out to the well alone and in the heat of the day (rather than earlier with other women) strongly suggests that she is not exactly in good standing with her own community. She comes across as someone with a mind of her own, with strength of character and yet an inherent vulnerability. Why has she had so many partners? And why is her present one not her sixth *husband?* Is she (as it used to be called) 'living in sin', or is she perchance having a relationship with an already married man? She is clearly searching for some kind of fulfilment and meaning in her life, and looking for that seems to carry more weight with her than the opinions of others as to how she is going about it.

Jesus soon picks up and pinpoints what is going on. And it is very instructive to note how he deals with the matter. Does he judge her, condemn her, give her a moral lecture, tell her to repent? No, he does none of these things. He indicates that he knows her situation, but when she quickly and adroitly changes the subject he doesn't pursue it. Instead, he does what in the culture of the time is unthinkable – he talks theology with a woman as with an equal. He treats her with respect and he tells her of the gracious, life-giving character of God. He meets her where she is and then follows her lead, knowing, surely, that by so doing there is the strongest likelihood that her life will be changed and she will at last recognise and embrace what she has been looking for.

What Jesus shares with her is of profound significance for everyone. He speaks of his gift of 'living water', which will become in those who drink it 'a spring of water gushing up to eternal life' (4:14). He tells her that true worship does not depend on being in a particular holy location but is a matter of worshipping God 'in spirit and truth' – that God, as well as being 'spirit', is personal enough to be addressed as 'Father' (4:20-24). And to this outsider woman of dubious reputation, and at her prompting, he reveals the truth about himself: 'The woman said to him, "I know that Messiah is coming ... When he comes, he will proclaim all things to us." Jesus said to her, "I am he, the one who is speaking to you"' (4:25, 26).

When the disciples return, the woman takes the opportunity to rush off (without her water jar!) and tell her community about her encounter. She becomes an evangelist. As a result, the Samaritans of Sychar city make their own acquaintance with Jesus. He readily agrees to stay with them for two more days (again, a less than proper thing for a Jew to do) and 'many more believed because of his word'. Their faith becomes direct: 'They said to the woman, "It is no longer because of what you said that we believe, for we have heard for ourselves, and we know that this is truly the Saviour of the world"' (4:41, 42).

Jesus' encounter with the Samaritan woman has thus become more than a personal conversation with an individual. It is a revelation of truth recognised by a community – and one which lies across the border from the land of the chosen people. In chapter 3 of John's Gospel, at the conclusion of Jesus' night-time meeting with Nicodemus, we are told that 'God so loved the world that he gave his only Son, so that everyone who believes in him may not perish but may have eternal life. Indeed, God did not send the Son into the world to condemn the world, but in order that the world might be saved through him' (3:16, 17).

The episode with the Samaritan woman and her community has started to flesh out that truth.

The woman taken in adultery (John 7:53–8:11)

This dramatic encounter, thrust upon Jesus by his opponents, seems to have proved problematic for the early Church. The narrative is something of a 'floating text', some manuscripts locating it at other points in John's Gospel, others placing it in Luke, and the earliest surviving manuscripts omitting it altogether. The likeliest explanation is that Jesus' approach to this situation caused some embarrassment (he did not condemn the adulterer), but the fact that the account was not fully suppressed strongly supports its historicity. The challenge was how to handle it.

It is important to remember that in Jesus' time and culture, adultery was a very serious offence. As the scribes and the Pharisees point out (setting a legal trap for Jesus), the penalty prescribed in the Jewish Law for a woman committing adultery was death by stoning. As they put it, their words clearly signalling their ulterior motive, 'Teacher, this woman was caught in the very act of committing adultery. Now in the law Moses commanded us to stone such women. Now what do you say?' (8:4, 5). John tells us what we have already guessed: 'They said this to test him, so that they might have some charge to bring against him' (8:6). To contradict the Law of Moses would certainly open him to condemnation. No genuine 'teacher' would ever do that. But they have a strong suspicion, from his reputation thus far, that Jesus will not be happy in this circumstance to affirm the Law's verdict. They therefore hope they have got him cornered.

And in the middle of all this, as convenient bait, is an anonymous woman. Her predicament is fraught with danger and shame. We can only imagine her feelings. Fear must surely be prominent among them. She is made to 'stand before all of them' – shamefully exposed as a sinner, and very probably in physical terms as well. She was 'caught in the very act' and is unlikely to have been given much time to make herself respectable. How her adultery was discovered is interesting to speculate (informers?). One thing is clear: only one party to the act has been dragged before Jesus. It normally takes two to commit adultery. So where is the man? The same Law which the scribes and Pharisees have cited makes it plain that a man in this situation is also culpable and, indeed, subject to the same penalty (see Leviticus 20 and Deuteronomy 22). In practice, as so often down the centuries, it is women who have to pay the price.

And how is this woman going to fare before a controversial teacher who, like her, is put on the spot? It is clear from his teaching that Jesus has what we might call a high view of marriage and a commitment to holy living. This is based not on observing legalities but on what he regards as fundamental principles, the purposes of God in creation. In another clash with the authorities, recorded in Mark 10, Jesus spells out his position. He quotes from Genesis 2:24: 'For this reason a man shall leave his father and mother and be joined to his wife, and the two shall become one flesh.' To this Genesis quotation, Jesus adds his own comments: 'So they are no longer two, but one flesh. Therefore what God has joined together, let no one separate.' Afterwards, alone with his disciples, Jesus makes some uncompromising remarks about remarriage and adultery (Mark 10:2-12).

Jesus has thus stated quite clearly God's best intentions for human marriage. And in a context where, as far as marriage is concerned, women are treated as property rather than as people, Jesus is giving a salutary reminder that, in the eyes of God, men and women are of equal value. Unfaithfulness on either side is an offence against one's partner. A woman is a person, not a piece of property.

Jesus also has some very challenging words to say about adultery: 'You have heard that it was said, "You shall not commit adultery." But I say to you that everyone who looks at a woman with lust has already committed adultery with her in his heart' (Matthew 5:27, 28). Who, then, can be saved?

On this test, applied honestly, every church congregation would contain not a few adulterers!

Is this perhaps the inner truth uncovered by Jesus when he says (eventually) to those who have accused the adulterous woman, 'Let anyone among you who is without sin be the first to throw a stone at her' (John 8:7)? There is something about this man that makes them realise they are not on safe territory. By challenging them to say they are sinless, he has exposed their hypocrisy and cornered them. The wisest thing is to leave the scene of their hoped-for triumph.

Jesus and the accused woman are now left to themselves. There is little doubt that she is guilty, and we might expect Jesus, with his extremely high moral standards, to remonstrate with her, making very clear to her the error of her ways. But not so. Instead he says to her, 'Woman, where are they? Has no one condemned you?'

'No one, sir,' she says.

To which Jesus responds, 'Neither do I condemn you.' Here is the real punchline of the encounter. The follow-up – 'Go your way, and from now on do not sin again' – is not a threat but an invitation to begin a new life (John 8:10, 11). Jesus by no means condones adultery, but he does not condemn her. It is the sin which is condemned, not the sinner.

God, above all, knows (and knows personally) the pain and damage caused by unfaithfulness. His response to that is Jesus, who came to seek and save the lost.

We do not know how the woman behaves after she goes on her way, but it would be strange indeed if this meeting with Jesus has not reached the heart of her. But, as ever, Jesus has left her with her own choice.

Though Jesus is uncompromising in his teaching about the sanctity of marriage, as we have seen from this and other encounters, his attitude and approach to individual failure are full of compassion, forgiveness and the possibility of new beginnings. God looks on the heart, not the outward appearance, and, on that basis, most people are fairly miserable failures. We all stand in need of forgiveness and the renewing grace of God. We can never fully live up to God's standards. God knows that. But God's response is not to condemn and punish. We see clearly from Jesus that the God of love knows that it is love that can change everything for the better, not condemnation. That kind of love is an enormous risk and can cost dearly. It cost Jesus his life. But it is the world's only hope.

It is not without significance that, from the evidence of all the Gospels, the harshest words of Jesus are reserved not for the 'failures' but for those who count themselves righteous, those ever ready to cast the first stone, those afflicted with chronic hardness of heart. We cannot get away from that – and we perhaps need the humility to learn from it. The woman caught in the act of adultery may help us to do so.

CHAPTER 5

Women in the teaching of Jesus

We have reflected so far on women who connected in some way with Jesus and his ministry. Again and again they have been signposts to the truth of God and the gospel. Female characters and imagery also feature significantly in Jesus' teaching. Clearly he feels that both women and men, in their lives and experiences, can be signs of the kingdom and pointers to the character of God. And equally clearly, as we shall see, Jesus himself has a 'feminine side'.

We turn now to that teaching of Jesus which features the experience of women. We look first at the female characters he includes. They occur mainly in the parables, those pithy, down-to-earth stories which Jesus so often uses to get across the character and workings of God. But there is also an interesting example tucked away in one of his clashes with the religious authorities. We begin with her.

The queen of the South (Matthew 12:42; Luke 11:31)

Faced with the hostile approaches of some of the scribes and Pharisees, Jesus is provoked into some strong responses which clearly (though not explicitly) point them to the significance of the one with whom they are taking issue. Within the period covered by Matthew 12, Jesus asserts to his opponents that 'something greater than the temple is here' (verse 6), 'something greater than Jonah is here' (verse 41) and 'something greater than Solomon is here' (verse 42). Though he is wise enough not to articulate this directly, the clear implication of what he is saying is that here in his person is someone who is more significant than the whole cultic system with its priesthood, more significant than the prophets who called people to repentance, and more significant even than Solomon, the epitome of wise kingship and the son of David. How shocking that must be to the guardians of holy tradition. This man is dangerous. He and his deluded claims have to be stopped before too many people are led astray.

It is in his riposte to his questioners that Jesus cites approvingly the example of the female ruler of a foreign country, who came to visit king Solomon to test out for herself his reputation for wisdom – 'the queen of the South', the queen of Sheba (verse 42). We find the account of her visit in 1 Kings 10:1-13. She was queen of the region of Sheba, somewhere in Arabia (precise location uncertain) and she came to see this other regional monarch with 'hard questions' and 'a very great retinue' (1 Kings 10:1, 2). She clearly wanted to make an impression, and one detects the distinct odour of monarchical rivalry! She herself was obviously not lacking in wealth or wit. But when she met and engaged with Solomon, she was, to put it colloquially, quite simply bowled over. 'There was no more spirit in her', we are told (1 Kings 10:4-5). She recognised Solomon's superior wealth and wisdom when it was in front of her.

Thus, says Jesus, many centuries later, this pagan queen can educate the teachers of Israel in a thing or two. Indeed, foreigner and woman though she be, she 'will rise up at the judgement with this generation and condemn it, because she came from the ends of the earth to listen to the wisdom of Solomon, and see, something greater than Solomon is here!' (Matthew 12:42).

This woman wanted to know the truth, took the initiative in seeking it out, and then acknowledged it when it stared her in the face. We do not need to possess wealth and power in order to follow her lead.

A woman making bread (Matthew 13:33; Luke 13:20, 21)
and women grinding meal (Matthew 24:41; Luke 17:35)

According to the Synoptic Gospels (not so much in John), one of Jesus' favourite means of communication was the parable – a little story making connections between the details of everyday life and the kingdom of God. Jesus was clearly acutely observant of the world around him and the way its inhabitants behaved. What he saw, he interpreted in his teaching as bearing messages from God.

His parables are vivid and memorable – not abstract theology but tales which bring home God's truth, God's encouragement and God's challenge. They would certainly have caught his listeners' attention, and their everyday details would have been readily recognised. Yet their meaning was by no means always crystal clear. The hearers were left to make of these stories what they would, to 'catch' the meaning for themselves. Further thought was required to work out what was hidden under the parable's surface. Any spelling out that Jesus did (as we see from Matthew 13) was shared with his committed disciples, not with his more general audience, and certainly not with his opponents, against whom a number of his parables were targeted. But these latter folk clearly got the message – and they did not like it.

Jesus evidently did not intend to do people's thinking for them. Excellent teacher that he was, he knew that we learn far more effectively if we tease things out for ourselves.

He also knew that that requires a willingness to do so, and that not everyone (not even among God's people) is prepared to engage in that way. It might prove too uncomfortable (again, see Matthew 13). Making the effort, however, can open up our understanding of God and how God works – even if it does challenge us to amend our lives!

The two 'cameo parables' we look at now are not so much stories as verbal paintings showing everyday scenes of female life at that time – baking bread and grinding meal. If we look attentively at these pictures, we may see more in them than immediately meets the eye. They relate to different points on the spectrum of God's kingdom: beginnings and endings, we might say.

The woman leavening the dough is adding to the mix something that will cause significant expansion. It is a hidden ingredient which in due course will bring about an evident result. So with the kingdom of heaven, suggests Jesus. To begin with, there may be little outward sign of it, but God is at work in the mix, and all will surely come to fruition at the proper time. God is the ultimate raising agent. But as with the Resurrection of Jesus, God often works wonders in the dark. And it is often only later that it dawns on us.

The woman baking bread, though, like God growing the kingdom, is well aware of what is going on and what the likely outcome will be. Tried and tested experience yields the expectation that what is hidden will have its transformative effect. Perhaps women, who know a little about growing hidden new life in the darkness of their own bodies, have a particular affinity with God in this regard. Certainly, as we shall see, Jesus also used imagery concerning women giving birth to point to spiritual realities.

Before we leave the industrious woman dealing with her baking, we might note that the amount of flour she is said to use would produce enough bread to feed a whole village. This has prompted not a little discussion. Is it perhaps indicating the grand scale of God's growing kingdom? Or did Jesus or the Evangelist get their measurements wrong? There is another possibility, which scholarly debate tends not to address. Was Jesus deliberately exaggerating to raise a smile? Not a few of his stories have a humorous dimension (see later on the parable of the judge and the widow). It seems he knew the educational value of making people chuckle – of making his stories somewhat larger than life.

When we look at the parabolic picture of the women grinding meal, we are in rather different territory. This is part of Jesus' teaching in Jerusalem during the week which would culminate in his crucifixion. It is to do with the 'end-time', the time when God will bring all things to their consummation and the Lord will return. The precise timing of this only God knows. It will happen suddenly, erupting in the midst of normal life, like the great flood of old, when folk are 'eating and drinking, marrying and giving in marriage' (Matthew 24:38). It will have a decisive and divisive effect, as God exercises final judgement. Of the two illustrative women routinely grinding their meal, 'one will be taken and one will be left' (Matthew 24:41). What that means exactly is (typically) not spelt out. But in some way, one will be saved and one will be lost. And the criterion for determining which fate awaits involves preparedness (Matthew 24:42-44).

Divine judgement is not a popular theme in this day and age (is it ever, except for fiery preachers?), but the teaching of Jesus is quite clear that, at some stage, there will be a final reckoning. And his picture of that happening while these women are going about their daily work is intended – quite literally – to bring the message home.

The lost coin (Luke 15:8-10)

Anyone who has lost something which is really valuable in every sense (a wedding ring, for example) will empathise with this woman!

The parable of the woman and her lost coin is placed by Luke between two other parables with a similar theme – that concerning a lost sheep (Luke 15:3-7) and a more extended story about a lost son (Luke 15:11-32). They were all prompted, Luke tells us, by the grumbling of the Pharisees and the scribes that Jesus was too fond of the company of undesirables. 'This fellow welcomes sinners and eats with them,' they complained (Luke 15:1, 2). The response of Jesus was to tell them these vivid and 'telling' parables, trying to get across to them that God cares intensely about those who have gone astray – and not just from a safe distance. God is a searching God. And when the lost are found, God's rejoicing knows no bounds. So the grumblers should stop their grumbling and get involved in God's mission.

The woman in the coin story is thus an indicator of what God is like. Her ten silver coins (literally, drachmas) are most probably her savings and/or dowry, possibly worn threaded on a string around her forehead, though this is not certain. However she may have stored them, one of them somehow has become lost. To her, this is a calamity. No doubt she is distressed at the loss because of the object's personal associations. But there must also be concern about the practical implications. This is a significant loss of resources, at least for her and her family. It is not clear what a drachma was worth at the time (probably about a day's wage for a labourer) but her reaction to losing it suggests that, to her, it matters a great deal.

Similarly, all *God's* resources, however humble, matter a great deal to God, both in themselves and in terms of the contribution they can make to the kingdom of love. The loss of just one provokes a determined search.

So it is with the woman. It is not an easy task, particularly in a house of that time with a low door and no windows – and no electricity. But she lights a lamp (so using up another valuable resource), and sweeps and searches diligently until she finds the coin. It counts that much. That, indeed, is brought home by her response. Not just relief but sheer joy. Joy that needs to be shared. The subsequent celebratory gathering of friends and neighbours must have been a memorable event!

That is also the case in heaven when one sinner repents. The angels have a party! And God delights in the restoration of a cherished loved one.

All 'grumblers', in whatever guise, take note.

The judge and the widow (Luke 18:1-8)

Christians believe that Jesus shows us what *God* is like. If that is true, then God undoubtedly has a well-developed sense of humour. The Gospel writings make it very clear that Jesus was a master at telling stories with a humorous twist – stories that would make people smile – and then make them think; vivid stories that often had a sharp sting in the tail. Bringing out the funny side of things can sometimes help to bring us face to face with home truths we would otherwise rather not look at.

The parable of the judge and the widow provides us with a very good example. Would that in those days there had been someone around with a smartphone so that we could have seen Jesus in action. The way he told it must have added greatly to the story's impact. But even the written words we are left with can give us some idea of how the story must have come across.

The purpose of the parable, as Luke explains to us (18:1), is to get across the 'need to pray always and not to lose heart.'

It is a vital message, and this memorable story has stood the test of time in encouraging people to hold to it.

One of the reasons it is so memorable is that in this little tale (as so often in his teaching), Jesus turns accepted ideas and prejudices on their heads. That becomes apparent when we look at the two characters in the story.

First there is the judge. Of course, people then as now expect judges to be concerned about justice and fair dealing; to be impartial and wise and beyond reproach. But, oh dear, *this* judge is none of those things. He neither fears God nor has any respect for his fellow human beings (18:2). He only cares about himself. He is the very opposite of what a judge should be.

And what about the widow? Now here is another turn-up for the books. In Jewish society of the time, women had very few legal rights. They belonged to their menfolk who had legal control over them. Women were not allowed to give evidence in a court of law because they were considered to be unreliable as witnesses. Widows were in an especially difficult position: in a culture where there were no state benefits, if they did not have a family willing to look after them, their situation was dire indeed.

Yet the widow-woman in this story turns out to be the one worthy of respect. It should be the judge, but instead it is one of this breed of allegedly unreliable women. *She* it is who shows strength, determination and persistence in the cause of justice.

Not for the first time, Jesus holds up a woman as a good example of faithful discipleship – and a feisty one at that.

Think about it, says Jesus. And think now about the sort of people you consider to be unreliable and not worthy of respect – and then think again. They might just have something to teach you.

In this story, the judge and the widow have an interesting relationship! The way it is described is really rather colourful, though this does not come across very strongly in our English translations. The judge cannot be bothered with this widow-woman. She is a pain in the neck, a disturbance of his self-centred peace. The widow knows this well enough but she refuses to give up. She shrewdly determines to exploit her nuisance value. Justice means more to her than fear of a lazy, selfish and corrupt judge. So she keeps coming and coming and coming, pestering and pestering and pestering. Put yourself in the judge's shoes, implies Jesus. How would you feel? Probably also exasperated by this wretched woman who will not go away.

But there is more. One translation (The New Jerusalem Bible) has the judge saying, 'I must give this woman her just rights since she keeps pestering me, or she will come and slap me in the face' (Luke 18:5). The literal meaning of that latter phrase is to give someone a black eye, or to beat them black and blue. As some might say nowadays, the judge is terrified of being 'handbagged' by the woman.

What a picture Jesus has painted! The frightened judge and the strong 'handbagging' woman. Designed to make the disciples laugh. Designed also to make them think. Because the one they have to learn from in the story is not the respected figure of the judge but the woman who has shattered the stereotype of weak vulnerability.

And *what* did they have to learn from her?

Not, perhaps, to 'handbag' God – who is not at all like the unjust judge in the story – but to be strong and confident and persistent in their praying – never to give up or lose heart, even when things seem very difficult. To keep on crying out to God, day and night. Crying out for what? Not to get their own way, not for an easy life – that is what the selfish judge wants. But, like the widow, they are to cry out for justice – for the coming of God's kingdom and God's values, into their own lives and the life of the world.

The same message still applies.

The wise and foolish maidens (Matthew 25:1-13)

Wedding imagery crops up in the teaching of Jesus on not a few occasions (see, for example, Mark 2:19, 20; Matthew 22:1-14; Luke 14:8-11). He evidently finds it helpful in conveying important messages about God's kingdom and his own significance within it. By clear implication, he is the Bridegroom, and his marriage feast (compare Revelation 19:9) is a splendid heavenly version of that messianic banquet, much anticipated at the time. The coming of God's kingdom is something to be celebrated, a cornucopia of God's loving generosity. Austerity is not a feature of heaven, it seems! It is no accident that when Jesus comes proclaiming the kingdom, he is regularly to be found 'eating and drinking' (Matthew 11:18, 19) at dinner-parties and feasts – and often with characters considered socially and religiously undesirable. Indeed, he is roundly criticised for such behaviour (Mark 2:15-17). But *God* is like that, says Jesus, bringing that message home both through his teaching and by the way he lives his life. God is a cause for rejoicing!

And so are weddings. The wedding at Cana in Galilee (John 2:1-11) must have been one of many attended by Jesus in his lifetime. Weddings were significant community events, not least in terms of inclusion and exclusion. Whether you were invited or not said much about your more general standing and acceptability within your community. Jesus will have observed what went on in and around these events with typical acuteness and with his spiritual antennae tuned for what they could say about God, and his own mission.

In the case of this parable, the theme of exclusion provides a chilling contrast to the overall context of rejoicing. The precise details of the part played by those who go to meet the bridegroom are not fully known to us, but the main thrust of the story is clear. The ten maidens go to do what is required of them. The five wise ones go prepared. The five foolish ones do not. The consequences are decisive for both groups.

'The readiness is all.' The context of that phrase in Shakespeare's *Hamlet* (Act 5, scene 2) may not be entirely auspicious, but its sentiment does neatly encapsulate the message of this somewhat terrifying parable.

Those who are 'ready' go with the bridegroom into the wedding banquet. But on those who are unready, 'the door was shut' (Matthew 25:10). What a fearful image. And it gets worse. Having managed, somehow, to replenish their oil supplies (waking the dealers up at midnight?), the foolish maidens return, saying, 'Lord, Lord, open to us.' They knock, but on this occasion, the door is *not* opened to them. Instead, they hear from the bridegroom those awful words, 'I do not know you' (Matthew 25:11, 12). They have been decisively disowned by the one in whose company they assumed they belonged. Insiders though they were, when the critical moment arrives, they are not ready – and they pay the price in exclusion and rejection.

On the face of it, this sounds disproportionately harsh. Surely their foolish unpreparedness does not merit such extreme judgement. But we need to recall the context. As Matthew presents it, this parable is part of a body of teaching delivered by Jesus in Holy Week, at the heart of a hostile religious establishment, as he approaches the greatest crisis of his life and ministry. Tension is high, and mounting. In this fraught atmosphere, much of his teaching, like this parable, relates to the cataclysmic event of God's ultimate reckoning, the timing of which God alone knows. It could be at any moment. In this setting, the unreadiness of the foolish maidens takes on a much more serious aspect.

What, then, is the character of that wise readiness that will open rather than close the door of heaven? Impacting as it does on our eternal destiny, this is rather more than an interesting academic question. We can perhaps best approach it by way of a *via negativa*, by establishing what it is not. That has already been trailed by Jesus at the climax of the Sermon on the Mount. As Jesus puts it then, near the beginning of his ministry, in a distinct echo of his later parable:

> 'Not everyone who says to me, "Lord, Lord", will enter the kingdom of heaven, but only one who does the will of my Father in heaven. On that day many will say to me, "Lord, Lord, did we not prophesy in your name, and cast out demons in your name, and do many deeds of power in your name?" Then I will declare to them, "I never knew you; go away from me, you evildoers."'
>
> *Matthew 7:21-23*

This is not immediately reassuring. You might think the folk mentioned above would be prime candidates for the kingdom of heaven. But performing religious activities, however powerful they might appear to be, will not, it seems, necessarily save those who do them. They are not in themselves a passport to heaven. Even those appointed to escort the bridegroom in joyful procession are not guaranteed a place at the feast.

Where, then, does this leave us (apart, perhaps, from feeling somewhat anxious and troubled, not least if we are 'insider' members of the community of faith)? Could we really be excluded at the last?

If nothing else, here is a divine wake-up call. Complacency and/or putting our trust in form rather than substance are both dangerous. As far as the values of God's kingdom are concerned, lip service will not do, however attractively executed. Something far deeper, far more demanding is required of God's people – something profoundly connected with the life and mission of God. As the psalmist puts it, the heart (that is, the very set of our will) needs to be ready (Psalm 108:1, *Book of Common Prayer*).

That means that, like the wise maidens, we need to make sure we always have reserves to draw on when we need them – spiritual reserves bolstered by a committed relationship with the Lord, which can be rekindled even in the darkness (Jesus on the cross is the ultimate example to us in this regard).

It is interesting (and perhaps encouraging) to note that in the parable, all the maidens, wise and foolish, fall asleep on their watch. When the critical moment of awakening comes, it is only the wise ones who have reserves and can immediately access them so that they can move on to fulfil their calling. It might be a worthwhile exercise, therefore, to ask ourselves what might be the state of our own spiritual reserves? Do we have any? In what do they consist and how do we seek to build them up? How do we draw on them when they are suddenly needed? Jesus, for example, in his great Calvary crisis, drew on the words of the Psalms, which he clearly knew by heart.

'The readiness is all.' But is this, after all, a counsel of despair? How on earth can we live up to such a requirement? We need to remember again that *all* the maidens fell asleep –

just like the three closest disciples of Jesus in the Gethsemane garden while he was enduring an agony of prayer. He had asked them to watch with him. They clearly could not manage it.

And there is more. Shortly after his teaching about the end-time, of which this parable is a part, Jesus shares a very significant supper with his disciples. He takes bread and breaks it. He takes wine and shares it. And he has a very painful conversation with Simon Peter, in the course of which, Peter says, 'Lord, I am ready to go with you to prison and to death!' But Jesus says, 'I tell you, Peter, the cock will not crow this day, until you have denied three times that you know me' (Luke 22:31-34).

'Lord, I am ready . . .' Yet just a few hours later, we hear Peter saying, 'I do not know the man!' (Matthew 26:74).

Mercifully, Jesus does not respond in like manner with that awful pronouncement from the parable: 'I do not know you.' What the Lord *knows* is that, despite Peter's abject failure, his claim of readiness came straight from his heart. He meant it, even though at the moment of testing he could not follow it through. So came radical forgiveness – and the rest, as they say, is history.

That should give us mighty encouragement. If our desire to be 'ready' for the Lord comes from the depths of our heart, heaven's door will never be shut on us, however feeble our service.

Female imagery in the teaching of Jesus

As well as including female *characters* in his teaching, Jesus also uses female *imagery*. Interestingly, that imagery is mostly motherly and domestic, and often to do with the processes of birth. Usually it refers to the experience of human women, but there is one significant instance where Jesus turns to the non-human feminine. Its very unexpectedness merits turning something of a reflective spotlight on it.

Jesus as 'mother hen'
(Luke 13:31-35; compare Matthew 23:37-39)

It is a cause of some sadness to the present author that the Bible makes no mention of domestic cats. There are lions, leopards and other fierce, wild beasts aplenty, but of the humble domestic moggy there is no sign. I cannot help thinking that this is a serious omission. However, all is not lost. Among the impressive and fearsome creatures featured in the Holy Scriptures, there lurk also those which are more homely and, indeed, more vulnerable – everyday creatures, which are both used and abused, valued and despised by that animal which bears the designation 'human'.

When we meet such creatures in the Gospels, they are invariably associated in some significant way with Jesus, whether as part of his teaching about God or in relation to the nature of his own person and mission. For Jesus, of course, the natural creation, in all its myriad and many-splendoured manifestations, carries vital messages from and about God. And that certainly includes those living beings, whether human or not, invariably considered too mundane to be worthy of very much serious attention. At Passiontide, two come into particular focus. First there is the donkey – load-bearer, often ill-treated labourer, in service to others yet with a stubborn will of its own, tough yet vulnerable. Then there is the lamb – fragile source of food and sacrifice. In a way that should affect us deeply, both animals point us to Jesus.

In the example from Luke's Gospel we are focusing on now, we are faced with another animal picture, no less affecting and, indeed, no less challenging. We might entitle this image, 'The fox and the hen'. Here are two traditional adversaries, in whose encounters the hen usually comes off worse! Yet Jesus calls Herod a fox and himself a hen. What is happening here? What are we to make of this?

We can perhaps readily understand why Jesus calls Herod a fox, risky though it undoubtedly is to do so. Herod is out to kill him – to eliminate the threat to both his power base and his conscience. It is what Herod does to those he takes against. And Jesus is far too closely linked with John the Baptist, who still haunts the tyrannical weakling who dispatched him. The image of the fox, then as now, was used as a byword for low and destructive cunning. Unfair though it might be to foxes, in using this image the message of Jesus is clear: Herod is an unpleasant and dangerous piece of work but he will not catch hold of Jesus. God's plan is that Jesus will fulfil the divine purpose in Jerusalem, where Herod has no jurisdiction, either geographically or spiritually. And even when the odds seem stacked up against it, God's plan will not be thwarted.

So why does Jesus describe himself as a hen, specifically as a mother hen? Surely an image of more evident strength and authority would be more appropriate at this point. Hens are taken out by foxes, not the other way round. This is not the kind of self-description we would expect from the self-expression of the living God.

But we must re-examine our apprehensions of divine power. The God of Jesus Christ always prevails, but not by brute strength. Though not by Herod, the one who describes himself as a hen is, in fact, savaged to death. It is an ignominious fate which, paradoxically and wonderfully, releases the extremity of God's love for the whole world and all that is in it – foxes included. Such love will never be destroyed, whatever is ranged against it.

And such love is achingly portrayed in the image of the *mother* hen. As used by Jesus, it is a beautiful picture – but also a tragic one. It speaks of motherly love, care and protection being both offered and spurned. If nothing else, it reveals something very important about Jesus that he can compare himself with such a common or garden creature, not least from his keen observation of its maternal habits. But there is more. In comparing himself to a mother hen, Jesus is also claiming imagery which in the Jewish Scriptures is used of God. God has already been pictured as a mother bird in the Old Testament: in the Psalms, for example, we find the composer praying, 'Hide me in the shadow of your wings' (Psalm 17:8) and again, 'All people may take refuge in the shadow of your wings' (Psalm 36:7). And perhaps most tellingly, in a psalm which is very familiar from the traditional Office of Compline, 'Thou shalt be safe under his feathers' (Psalm 91:4, *Book of Common Prayer*).

It is no less than God, of whom Jesus is the incarnation, who longs that his beloved children should scurry to him for love and warmth and protection. What an amazing longing. What an amazing offer. And how utterly tragic it is for all concerned – God included – when that offer is spurned. There are few more acutely painful verses in the New Testament than the one we find here: 'How often would I have gathered your children together as a hen gathers her brood under her wings, and you would not' (Luke 13:34, RSV). 'And you would not.' The hurt in Jesus' voice, and even more in his heart, is surely indescribable.

What of us? As God's beloved children, we, too, are urged to shelter and snuggle under God's feathers. And we, too, have a choice. Though Love will use all its persuasive powers, Love will never force us where we do not want to go. If we so choose, we can scuttle to and fro regardless around our own little patch, easy prey for any and every stray fox. What a waste, in every sense, that would be.

We should not be too proud to be as children with God. As Jesus said, unless we become as little children, we shall not enter the kingdom of heaven (Matthew 18:3; Mark 10:15). Especially when we are afraid or in any way threatened, especially when our hearts are crying out for tender loving care, especially when we feel lost and lonely, tired and traumatised – or just in need of a reassuring embrace – we should make straight for God and bury ourselves in the ever-available warmth of his love for us – at all times and in all places. That is precisely what God is longing for us to do, so there is no need to be embarrassed.

Institutional embarrassment is perhaps one of the reasons why the Gospel image of Jesus as mother hen has not been taken up very much in liturgy and tradition. Some leading Christian figures have pursued it, however, and the insight of one in particular is worthy of an extended quotation. We notice in that quotation, incidentally, that in using this maternal imagery of Jesus, the masculine pronoun is retained. There is no suggestion that Jesus should be deprived of his historical gender! Jesus himself, in using this imagery, was man enough (and God enough) to know that the comprehensive nature of divine love transcends all gender divisions and stereotypes. What matters is that this love should be understood and experienced. Whatever imagery can bring this about is thus to be unashamedly embraced.

Anselm, eleventh-century archbishop of Canterbury and one of the leading theologians and thinkers of all Christian history, also knew this. What follows is taken from one of his prayers and meditations (from *Prayer to St Paul*). Can we identify with his prayer?

And you, Jesus, are you not also a mother?
Are you not the mother who, like a hen,
gathers her chickens under her wings?

And you, my soul, dead in yourself,
run under the wings of Jesus your mother
and lament your griefs under his feathers.
Ask that your wounds may be healed
and that, comforted, you may live again.

Christ, my mother,
you gather your chickens under your wings;
this dead chicken of yours puts himself under those wings.
For by your gentleness the badly frightened are comforted,
by your sweet smell the despairing are revived,
your warmth gives life to the dead,
your touch justifies sinners.

Mother, know again your dead [child],
both by the sign of your cross and the voice of his confession.
Warm your chicken, give life to your dead [child],
justify your sinner.
Let your terrified one be consoled by you;
despairing of himself, let him be comforted by you;
and in your whole and unceasing grace
let him be refashioned by you.

For from you flows consolation for sinners;
to you be blessing for ages and ages. Amen.[3]

Amen, indeed.

Human female imagery in the teaching of Jesus

In the Synoptic Gospels, Jesus' use of human female imagery is largely to be found in his teaching about the cataclysmic events that will accompany the time of God's coming judgement. Though the picture he paints is not crystal clear in terms of detail and process, the fear and anguish this time will evoke come across starkly and vividly. As Jesus puts it, 'Woe to those who are pregnant and to those who are nursing infants in those days!' (Matthew 24:19; Mark 13:17). He is aware of their special vulnerability and uses this as an illustration of the severe challenges God's judgement will bring.

There will be tumult and turbulence, 'nation will rise against nation, and kingdom against kingdom, and there will be famines and earthquakes in various places' – but, says Jesus, 'all this is but the beginning of the birth pangs' (Matthew 24:7, 8; see also Mark 13:8). The seismic upheavals which will precede the arrival of the end are compared to labour pains. Undoubtedly, Jesus would be well aware of the writhing, gasping and screaming associated with women giving birth. He was brought up in a small town, in an age when home birth was the only option and there were few aids to alleviate the pain. Giving birth was both a noisy and a risky process. Jesus would certainly have heard what went on.

But he would also be aware that this imagery has been used by prophets before him to speak of the sufferings brought

---

3. *The Prayers and Meditations of Saint Anselm*, Penguin Classics, 1973, pp.155-6.

by times of crisis. Isaiah, for example, says this of the people of Babylon, as he looks to the time of reckoning that will be brought upon them: 'Pangs and agony will seize them; they will be in anguish like a woman in labour' (Isaiah 13:8). Jeremiah uses the same image to portray the experience of the people of Jerusalem as they face the onslaught of an enemy: 'We have heard news of them, our hands fall helpless; anguish has taken hold of us, pain as of a woman in labour' (Jeremiah 6:24). And this from Micah, foretelling defeat and exile for the people of Zion: 'Writhe and groan, O daughter Zion, like a woman in labour; for now you shall go forth from the city and camp in the open country; you shall go to Babylon' (Micah 4:10).

The sufferings of women at this critical time in their experience have thus long been thought a fitting comparator to painful times of crisis in human experience more generally. Jesus takes up that tradition. But that leaves us with a crucial question. All being well, labour pains lead to the emergence of new life. How does that sit with their use as imagery which seems entirely negative and suggestive of a fearful outcome?

In the case of Jesus, we have some indicators of a positive way through this dilemma. Towards the climax of his ministry, Jesus has a significant little exchange with Peter, who, speaking on behalf of all the disciples, says to him, 'Look, we have left everything and followed you. What then will we have?' Jesus responds to this hardly selfless approach with the following words: 'Truly I tell you, at the renewal of all things, when the Son of Man is seated on the throne of his glory, you who have followed me will also sit on twelve thrones, judging the twelve tribes of Israel' (Matthew 19:27, 28). The word translated by the NRSVA as 'renewal' literally means regeneration or rebirth. It seems that Jesus believes that the labour pains of the end-time will indeed issue in a new beginning – a new genesis for God's world. The suffering, though all too real, will not be in vain, nor will it be entirely destructive. And the followers of Jesus will enjoy the benefits of this vibrant new life.

John's Gospel helps us to explore this further. We learn there that on the night before he is crucified, the same night in which he is betrayed, Jesus shares a special time with his disciples, seeking to prepare them for what is to come. What he says to them is clearly infused with love and encouragement. It is also profound – so much so that the disciples find it difficult to understand. At one point, they discuss it *sotto voce* amongst themselves, not able to bring themselves to ask Jesus about it directly. But, as ever, Jesus knows what is going on and he addresses their bewilderment head on. In doing so, he turns to an image from everyday life which would surely speak to them clearly in their confusion and fear. He says to them:

> 'Are you discussing among yourselves what I meant when I said, "A little while, and you will no longer see me, and again a little while, and you will see me"? Very truly, I tell you, you will weep and mourn, but the world will rejoice; you will have pain, but your pain will turn into joy. When a woman is in labour, she has pain, because her hour has come. But when her child is born, she no longer remembers the anguish because of the joy of having brought a human being into the world. So you have pain now; but I will see you again, and your hearts will rejoice, and no one will take your joy from you.'
>
> *John 16:19-22*

The death of Jesus will indeed bring great distress and anguish to the disciples. There will be no getting away from that. And in the midst of it, there will seem to be no way out. But Easter will bring new life and joy beyond all telling. In fact, in a telling twist to the image, they themselves will be newly born.

Much earlier in his ministry, Jesus uses the language of new birth with another confused enquirer. The Pharisee Nicodemus comes to Jesus 'by night' – under cover of darkness, so as not to be seen, but also in darkness of understanding. What Jesus tries to get him to 'see', to begin with at least only causes him further confusion. Jesus says to him, 'Very truly, I tell you, no one can see the kingdom of God without being born from above' (John 3:3).

As his response shows, this fazes Nicodemus completely: 'How can anyone be born after having grown old? Can one enter a second time into the mother's womb and be born?' (John 3:4).

Jesus goes on to explain that entering into the kingdom of God involves a spiritual rebirth – 'being born of water and Spirit' (John 3:5). The fluids of this birth tap directly into the life of God.

Jesus will talk further in his ministry about God's 'living water' and God's Spirit of truth, and, indeed, the close association between them (see, for example, John 4:7-15; 7:37-39; 14:15-17). And in the fourth Gospel, his own death is presented as the means of new birth into God's kingdom: when the body of Jesus is pierced, 'at once blood and water came out' (John 19:34). In dying, Jesus releases the very life of God, available to all who hold to him in faith. As John puts it in his Prologue, 'to all who received him, who believed in his name, he gave power to become children of God, who were born, not of blood or of the will of the flesh or of the will of man, but of God' (John 1:12, 13).

As in the Synoptics, though in a very different way, this birth imagery in John is associated with God's judgement.

That judgement is to be seen focused on the cross. As Jesus puts it, shortly before he is 'lifted up' (that is, both exalted and crucified), 'Now is the judgement of this world; now the ruler of this world will be driven out. And I, when I am lifted up from the earth, will draw all people to myself' (John 12:31, 32). In John's Gospel, divine judgement is in every sense the exposure of truth – and the crux of this matter is indeed to be found in Jesus stripped naked on the cross. Here is exposed the truth of God (absolute love and forgiveness made flesh in Jesus); here is laid bare the reality of evil (the forces of darkness looking to have their day); and here, for good or ill, the secrets of many hearts are revealed. And out of all this, it is God who prevails. The God of love. The God who ever strives to bring forth new life, even struggling and writhing to do so on a cross. Indeed, it is God who labours with us. It is this committed love which is triumphant, causing Jesus to cry out at the end, 'It is accomplished' (John 19:30 – 'finished' is far too negative a translation).

The travail will produce its fruit. And in this understanding, the cross (and by extension the judgement of God) ceases to be primarily a thing of horror. It is a supreme expression of love which draws people into God's presence, there to find acceptance, forgiveness and renewal, not to say eternal life. As Jesus put it (see John 6:37), 'anyone who comes to me I will never drive away'.

Anyone. Yet, of course, even absolute love can be spurned. What happens then, not least at the final reckoning, remains in the hands of God.

CHAPTER 6

What has this to do with us?

What has all this to do with us? To reapply a phrase from St Paul (Romans 3:2), much, in every way. Whoever we are, whether female or male, God can touch us, and we can touch God, through the women featured in this book.

In our reflections on them, the relevance of these women to the life of faith today has surfaced again and again. As the author of Hebrews might have put it, though they have died, they still speak (Hebrews 11:4). What they say can have a significant impact on us, expressed in many and various ways. As with Scripture as a whole, the Holy Spirit can take their 'there and then' and apply it powerfully to our 'here and now'. And however many times we turn to look at these women, there will always be something more to discover and take to heart.

Pray God, readers will have gone on their own journeys with Jesus' women. In this concluding chapter, we shall simply try to highlight some of the overarching themes which have become apparent through the preceding reflections.

We may note, first, the sheer diversity of the women we encounter in the Gospels. They do indeed comprise 'all sorts and conditions' (to use the language of a traditional *BCP* prayer). They cover a whole range of backgrounds, personalities and circumstances. Jesus' women are not monochrome or stereotypical. They speak for themselves. They are their own persons. And they all relate, in one way or another, to a Jesus who allows them to be so. The Lord tends to sit light to cultural and religious expectations. He enables (and not infrequently provokes) people, both women and men, to be who they truly are.

This Jesus 'is the same yesterday and today and for ever' (Hebrews 13:8). One important lesson to take on board, therefore, is that people of all shapes and sizes (in every sense of that phrase!) are welcome to be who they are in the Lord's presence. God delights in diversity. There is no holy mould into which we have to fit to be acceptable to God.

Jesus' women certainly bring that message home. In all their diversity, whenever and however these varied women came into contact with Jesus, something good happened: from women of high status in society (like the wife of Herod's steward) to those leading respectable ordinary lives (like Martha and Mary); from those with material wealth (like those who ministered to Jesus of their substance) to those living in poverty (like the widow and her sacrificial offering); from those frowned upon by the establishment (like prostitutes and the woman caught in the act of adultery) to those on the fringes of acceptability (like the woman with an issue of blood) to those who were considered undeserving outsiders (like the woman of Samaria and the Syrophoenician woman).

This is a salutary reminder to us that the purposes of the God of love, made flesh in Jesus, are entirely positive. God passionately desires what is best for the whole of creation. In a world lovingly given true freedom, this means that God has to labour to bring forth divine love in and through life as it is – life in all its wonder, failure, joy and heartbreak. Anyone and everyone is invited to be God's midwife in this respect, delivering God's love in many and various ways. As Jesus' women have shown us, perfection is not a required qualification – and that includes moral perfection. Of course, God does not sanction immoral behaviour (any more than God sanctions any other kind of sin), but God also sees the potential for true love in people and is determined to try and draw it out. Not a few of the women associated with Jesus illustrate that perfectly!

Indeed, when we look at the working out of God's plan through the whole of Scripture, we see how frequently it involves readily incorporating the less than good, redeeming what is often highly unpromising material in order to move forward God's will. That commitment has its supreme expression in Jesus on the cross. Nothing could seem more hopeless, and yet it is hope's apex, hope's 'finest hour' – the definition and the triumph of real love.

As we stand with Jesus' women at Golgotha, that reality may have opportunity to penetrate the soul more deeply.

The diverse women we have looked at come into contact with Jesus in all sorts of ways. Sometimes it is not asked for and Jesus takes the initiative (as with the widow of Nain), but often the women themselves make some kind of approach. That could be verbal or non-verbal. The words they use are words of challenge, wit and intelligence, as well as beseeching. Many of these women have no hesitation in confronting Jesus in the sharpest of terms (Martha and the Syrophoenician woman, for example). And in his responses, Jesus takes their words as his cue for dialogue. He respects what they say and engages with them on their own ground. So with us – not least when we have painful questions in our hearts. Plain speaking hits home with the God of truth.

The women's non-verbal communication is expressed in telling body language. There are tears (Mary of Bethany, Luke's anointing woman, the daughters of Jerusalem, Mary Magdalene) and there is touch (the woman with an issue of blood, the anointing women, Mary Magdalene in the Resurrection garden). And there is being in the presence of

Jesus and letting their bodies speak for them (the woman bent double, his mother and the other women at the scene of the crucifixion). These are powerful expressions of prayer still open to us. Though we do not have the privilege of seeing Jesus in the flesh, we can 'see Jesus' (Hebrews 2:9) with our spiritual imagination and so pursue our agenda with him in whatever way we feel most helpful or necessary. Letting our bodies do the talking can often be our most eloquent and effective prayer. We should not be shy of that. Jesus' women can give us confidence in that regard.

Jesus, of course, ministers to the women he encounters in ways appropriate for them. But it is important to note that, on not a few occasions, the 'ministry' is mutual. The women receive much from Jesus, but he also receives much from them. That is true *par excellence* in relation to his mother, Mary. She nurtured him in her womb and brought him into the world. She loved and protected him through his childhood (not least when he was under real physical threat as an infant), and she was no doubt responsible for much of his learning in his formative years. Did she share with him any of her ponderings? It would be fascinating to know. When he grew up, though the relationship was sometimes ambivalent and edgy, Mary continued to contribute to his understanding of his mission, as the episode at Cana clearly shows. And at the end, she is standing there, giving him support in the only way she can. How Jesus responds to this *in extremis* says just how much it means to him. His disciples could not watch with him one brief hour. She is there when it matters.

Before that black yet good Friday, Jesus also received tender loving care from women who truly cared about him and were sensitive to his needs. Jesus was a real human being, with real emotions and susceptibility to hurt and pain. His humanity came under increasing stress and attack as he made his difficult way to his great crisis in Jerusalem. How much, then, he must have appreciated the ministrations of those who loved him, especially perhaps the bold and extravagant actions of those women who anointed him. They provided balm for his body and soul. In the midst of hostility and lack of understanding, they touched him with a tenderness for which his heart must have yearned.

And we should not forget those women who enabled his ministry, both in terms of finance and practicalities and of personal support and encouragement. Their ministry to him was surely vital.

Just as Jesus still ministers to us in our need, through many and various agents, so is he still, in any number of guises, in need of our ministry. As he said in one of his most challenging parables, 'Truly I tell you, just as you did it to one of the least of these who are members of my family, you did it to me' (Matthew 25:40). Whenever and however we bring love, tenderness, support and enabling to those in need of them, we minister also to Jesus. What a privilege that is.

And it is a privilege still to be able to meet the women in Jesus' earthly life, through the imprint they have left on Scripture. They are fascinating people in themselves. They also point us to Jesus. And they have much yet to say, even to our day and age. May they continue to make their mark on us.

Other books Joy has written or contributed to for Kevin Mayhew:

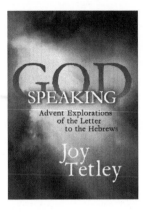

God Speaking
Advent Explorations of the Letter to the Hebrews
1501477

Facing the Issues
A Christian approach to Moral Dilemmas, Social Concerns and Relationships
1501353

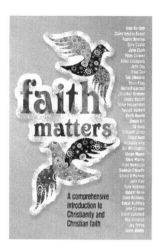

Faith Matters
A comprehensive introduction to Christianity and Christian faith
1501369

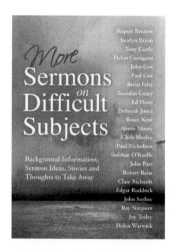

More Sermons on Difficult Subjects
Background information, sermon ideas,
stories and thoughts to take away
1501389
Also available: Sermons on Difficult Subjects: 1501299